CW00537898

Praise for
Win with Proven Stock Selection and Market Timing Tools

"This new book by Gerald Appel follows the rich legacy he has established over the years; it is a treasure chest of valuable advice which bestows on the reader the benefit of his decades of investment experience. It receives my highest recommendation."

—Edward D. Dobson, President, Traders Press

BEAT THE MARKET

WIN WITH PROVEN STOCK SELECTION AND MARKET TIMING TOOLS

BEAT THE MARKET

WIN WITH PROVEN STOCK SELECTION AND MARKET TIMING TOOLS

GERALD APPEL

Vice President, Publisher: Tim Moore
Associate Publisher and Director of Marketing: Amy Neidlinger
Executive Editor: Jim Boyd
Editorial Assistants: Pamela Boland and Myesha Graham
Operations Manager: Gina Kanouse
Digital Marketing Manager: Julie Phifer
Publicity Manager: Laura Czaja
Assistant Marketing Manager: Megan Colvin
Cover Designer: R&D&Co
Managing Editor: Kristy Hart
Project Editor: Todd Taber
Copy Editor: Water Crest Publishing, Inc.
Proofreader: Paula Lowell
Senior Indexer: Cheryl Lenser
Senior Compositor: Gloria Schurick
Manufacturing Buyer: Dan Uhrig

Publishing as FT Press
Upper Saddle River, New Jersey 07458

This book is sold with the understanding that neither the author nor the publisher is engaged in rendering legal, accounting or other professional services or advice by publishing this book. Each individual situation is unique. Thus, if legal or financial advice or other expert assistance is required in a specific situation, the services of a competent professional should be sought to ensure that the situation has been evaluated carefully and appropriately. The author and the publisher disclaim any liability, loss, or risk resulting directly or indirectly, from the use or application of any of the contents of this book.

FT Press offers excellent discounts on this book when ordered in quantity for bulk purchases or special sales. For more information, please contact U.S. Corporate and Government Sales, 1-800-382-3419, corpsales@pearsontechgroup.com. For sales outside the U.S., please contact International Sales at international@pearson.com.

Printed in the United States of America

First Printing December 2008

ISBN-10: 0-13-235917-0
ISBN-13: 978-0-13-235917-7

Pearson Education LTD.
Pearson Education Australia PTY, Limited.
Pearson Education Singapore, Pte. Ltd.
Pearson Education North Asia, Ltd.
Pearson Education Canada, Ltd.
Pearson Educación de Mexico, S.A. de C.V.
Pearson Education—Japan
Pearson Education Malaysia, Pte. Ltd.

Library of Congress Cataloging-in-Publication Data

Appel, Gerald.

Beat the market—win with proven stock : selection and market timing tools / Gerald Appel.
p. cm.

ISBN 0-13-235917-0 (hbk. : alk. paper) 1. Investments. 2. Speculation. 3. Portfolio management. I. Title.

HG4521.A636 2009

332.63'22--dc22

2008026062

This book is dedicated to my grandchildren,
Emily, Caroline, and Alexandra,
who bring so much life and love to wherever they go...

Contents

ACKNOWLEDGMENTS

Although *Beat the Market—Win with Proven Stock Selection and Market Timing Tools* has been structured to be a rather straightforward and brief work, its lessons have actually been culled from the studies, experiences, and conclusions of many astute and serious students of the behavior of the stock and bond markets, as well as from my own more than forty years' experience as a personal stock trader, investment advisor, and money manager for the accounts of hundreds of investors.

The roster of people from whom I have learned is far too long to list in these pages, but I do want to extend my particular appreciation to Ned Davis and the staff of Ned Davis Research, Inc., who have provided so very many ideas, data, and research material to myself and to other investors over the years and who have been very generous in allowing my use of publication material in books that I have written.

Dr. Martin E. Zweig, a legendary technical analyst, student of the market, and investment manager, has been a source of many useful concepts to myself and to so many others. Yale Hirsch remains the primary expert regarding the influences of seasonal cycles on the behavior of stocks and bonds.

A bit closer to home, I would like to express my appreciation to Glenn Gortler, the Director of Research at my company, Signalert Corporation, as well as to Joon Choi, Roni Greiff Nelson, Bonnie Gortler, Joanne Quan Stein, and Arthur Appel—members of the portfolio and research staff at Signalert—for their ideas and editorial assistance.

My son, Dr. Marvin Appel, Ph.D., has emerged over the years as a pre-eminent market expert, particularly in investment strategies that may be applied to exchange-traded funds (ETFs). If I have taught him anything during his development, he has more than returned the favor in the years that he and I have been working together.

And, as usual, I owe no one more than I owe the mother of my children and wife of 52 years, Judith Appel. In my very first book, *Winning Market Systems*, written in 1971, I referred to Judy as my best investment. Now, 37 years later, she remains my very best long-term holding.

Gerald Appel

About the Author

Gerald Appel has, since 1973, published *Systems and Forecasts*, a leading technical analysis publication. He is legendary for his work in technical analysis and market timing, including the creation of Moving Average Convergence/Divergence (MACD), one of the field's most valuable tools. His books include *Opportunity Investing*, *Winning Market Systems*, and *Technical Analysis—Power Tools for Active Investors*. His company, Signalert, with its affiliates, currently manages approximately $250,000,000 in private capital. He has trained thousands of traders through his renowned tapes, seminars, and workbooks.

INTRODUCTION

I am going to begin this book with a promise.

I believe that most readers of this book will be able to complete it within two to three weeks. This work has been purposely left short of philosophy, fluff, and filler. Its content is dense with instruction, theoretical and actual performance results, tactics, and strategies that you can employ immediately.

If you do your part—that is, to complete the reading and to work through the examples within—you will emerge from the process with all the information you should need to become a savvy and highly successful investor for years to come.

You will learn to recognize when stocks should be bought, when they should be held, and when they should be sold.

The Weekly Market Power Gauge

You will learn readily followed, easy-to-understand, and efficient stock market indicators associated with general levels of interest rates that will help you identify those periods when stocks are very likely to advance in price, when they are only just likely to advance in price, when you might just as well stay home, and when staying home with your capital is likely to be an excellent idea.

You will also learn an indicator that is designed to identify, by just one weekly indicator of stock market performance, the time when prices are likely to continue to rise for weeks—often even for months—with a high probability of accuracy. The best gains in the stock market occur when this indicator is in effect. At other times, gains tend to be more limited.

The combination of these indicators may be taken to reflect the Weekly Market Power Gauge. When the gauge is indicating unanimous strength in the indicators you follow, the odds very heavily favor being in stocks. Low readings in the gauge suggest caution.

In other words, you will learn how and when to put the probabilities on your side—to invest when risks are the least and to recognize when risks are the greatest.

You will also learn how to build your stock portfolio—what to buy and what not to buy—and how to blend the components of your portfolio in such a way that the whole is better performing than the average of its parts, as well as how to select mutual funds and exchange traded funds that are most likely to outperform the average stock, fund, or exchange-traded fund.

I cannot promise profit on each and every trade. I can promise, however, that you will have put at your own disposal, the ability to invest objectively, to invest with a plan and strategy, and to invest, over the long term, very successfully.

Demystifying the Process of Investing...

If you are reading this book, there is a good chance that you at least occasionally tune in to those television programs on CNBC, Bloomberg, or elsewhere that feature up-to-the-minute stock market reports, intermixed with streams of market experts—with sometimes up to four or even six heads at a time, and usually with a bullish bias—who agree or disagree regarding prospects for the stock market, near and long term.

Given the constraints of television time, experts are provided with one or perhaps a few minutes to succinctly stake out their positions. For the most part, Wall Street pundits tend to be optimistic—particularly corporate representatives, who, naturally, have their own stakes in expressing optimism regarding their own industries or companies, or executives of mutual funds, who are most unlikely to advise investors to bail out of the stock market.

Still, you might wonder—with all those computers available, with all those financial and technical wizards in-house, and with all that research data at hand—why so few market forecasts are in agreement, and to the extent that they are, it is usually to the effect that what has been happening in the marketplace is what will continue to happen.

Perhaps there are too many experts, too much information, too many indicators—much of which is contradictory—and too much implied need to predict what may happen in the future rather than to simply respond to what is taking place in the present. You will be learning just a few indicators: tools and techniques by which you can track the stock market—not by forecasting weeks, months, or years ahead, but simply by being able to recognize when it is time to hop aboard the train, as well as recognizing when it is time to exit the party.

The tools that you will learn are the basic tools that I employ to manage my own and my clients' money.

Money is serious business. Other people's money is even more serious. If you know your clients personally, the way my company tries to know its clients, you know the importance of accumulating for the time when you can no longer work, you understand the seriousness of late-life illness when cash on hand is insufficient for medical expenses, and you learn the impact of inflation on lifetime nest eggs.

I, my son, and our staff take investing very seriously. I have personally spent a good part of my lifetime studying, researching, and testing methods by which investment results may be improved. You will be learning strategies by which large amounts of actual clients' money—and my own—are being invested.

This is not a large book. I have written it to be a serious book.

I promised a brief but useful work.

Let's cut to the chase.

Gerald Appel

PROLOGUE

A Signal for a New Bull Market Is Given...

The time is September 6, 2002. The stock market is in the final throes of one of the most vicious bear markets in history—a bear market that has already taken the Standard & Poor's Index down by 47% from its early 2000 peak levels, and which has lopped 77% from the Nasdaq Composite Index.

Pessimism is rampant. Investors have seen serious damage done to their personal savings, to their retirement plans, and to their asset base in general. Many mutual funds have shut down or merged. A war with Iraq looms on the horizon, adding to the general uncertainty.

However, two indicators—indicators that measure the value of stocks compared to the values of alternative investments—flash the all-clear signals that the time has come to enter into the stock market with full force; signals that stocks are once again bargains; signals to buy and to buy now!

And, as matters turned out, these proved to be very timely signals, indeed. The buy signals that these two indicators produced on September 6, 2002, were followed by a market advance that did not come to an end until October 9, 2007. At that time, the Standard & Poor's 500 Index had risen from 893.92 to 1565.15—a gain of 671 points or 75.1%.

However, by July 13, 2007, three months before the final peak, trouble had begun to appear on Wall Street. A rash of defaults in the mortgage industry had spread to financial institutions across the globe as it became apparent that lenders had extended far too much credit to far too many borrowers who did not have the capacity to repay. As the financial community reeled, losses mounting as a result of a rash of defaults—with major institutions, such as Citicorp, ultimately losing half their value—the stock market turned down, losing 9.4% in just four weeks.

What were the indicators that had placed investors into the stock market in 2002 suggesting at this juncture? They steadfastly retained their bullish status, maintaining their favorable outlook throughout the July–August 2007 decline. This optimism was rewarded as the Standard & Poor's 500 Index recovered to new highs on October 9, less than two months after the lows of August.

The past history of these "value indicators" had been marked by stock market declines of up to 17%, even while their status remained favorable. These measures of stock market value were not designed for in-and-out trading but rather to alert investors as to when stocks represented or no longer represented favorable value. History has shown that when stocks are still "inexpensive," market declines do not last for very long.

Following the October recovery, which brought many popular market indices to new all-time highs, pessimism quickly returned, with subsequent market declines reaching the area of 18% in January 2008—still barely within but threatening to violate past boundaries of risk.

However, stocks DID recover, after one final dip in March, reclaiming by mid-May most of the losses taken at the start of the year.

As matters had turned out, the stock market had found support within the normal range of market fluctuation implied by the indicator set that had called, with such accuracy, the end of the bear market, and had kept its followers in stocks all through the 2002–2008 period. These indicators had been bent by the "sub-prime credit crisis." However, they did not break.

The two indicators that measure stock market value have been combined into one key indicator: the "Twin Bond–Stock Valuation Model," which has been generating accurate signals since 1981. You will learn in this book all you need to know to assess the stock market by way of this timing model so that you, too, can identify key market turning points of the sort that took place during September 2002.

Please join me as we explore the procedures involved.

Gerald Appel
July 2008

CHAPTER 1

YOUR BASIC INVESTMENT STRATEGY

Successful investment in the stock market involves a major decision: what ***to buy***.

Should you buy individual stocks, mutual funds, or exchange traded funds (ETFs—recently developed hybrids of stocks and mutual funds)? Should you be investing in domestic stocks, in stocks and/or mutual funds that represent markets overseas, in large company issues, in smaller company issues, in technology companies, or in higher-yielding financial corporations? And, even more difficult—which stocks, which mutual funds, or which ETFs should you consider?

These decisions sound complicated—but, luckily, there are strategies that you will learn that should almost certainly, almost ***automatically***, put your capital in the right place at the right time, including cash when general stock market conditions are unlikely to favor the ownership of stocks. These strategies—which are ***not complicated*** to apply—are discussed in the final portions of this book.

Although the selection of your individual investment holdings is of significance, of probably more significance is the general direction of the various stock markets—domestic and foreign—in which you might invest. For the most part, when the stock market as a whole is strong, the average stock is likely to rise in price, particularly if you invest via broadly based mutual funds, which are more likely to represent the "stock market" than individual stocks.

In other words, if you invest only during periods of generally rising stock prices, the odds are going to be heavily on your side that you ***will outperform*** the general stock market—all the more so if you apply successful techniques for the selection of your investments. If you place all or at least a significant amount of your investment capital on the sidelines—earning safe interest flows—during periods of market uncertainty or weakness, you will be able to ***reduce risk and preserve*** your capital while other investors are achieving only minimal gains or actually taking losses.

I will show you, in the first section of this book, some simple but highly effective techniques for assessing the likely strength of the stock market that have, over more than a quarter of a century, ***proven to be successful*** in determining when stocks have represented good investments and when it has been safer to just maintain cash positions.

Believe it or not, you should be able to maintain and to ***apply these market-timing techniques*** that will show you when to be invested, as well as those strategies for picking the best places in which to invest, in ***probably less than one or two hours per week***.

The Best and Worst Mindsets for Profitable Investing

Let's consider some of the mindsets that investors fall into that really work against making money in the investment markets—mindsets that you do ***not*** want to have.

Paying Too Much Attention to What the "Experts" Are Saying

The simple fact of the matter is that market newsletters, financial columnists, and guests on television financial newscasts tend to frequently contradict each other, frequently follow rather than lead the stock and bond markets in their outlooks, and tend to be wrong when, as a group, they are overwhelmingly either bullish or bearish relating to the stock market.

Relatively few stock market advisory letters have had histories of actually outperforming buy-and-hold strategies in real-time investing. For that matter, the majority of mutual funds have not succeeded in this regard as well.

You should keep in mind that the stock market ***tends to discount news***, rising and/or falling not in response to news that has already been released but rather to news that savvy investors ***anticipate being released*** in the near or long-term future. By the time magazines, television, radio, and the web have already started to promote a particular issue or market sector—generally after large gains have already been achieved in these areas—it is too late to take safe positions.

Remember: The financial press is usually the most bearish at or near market bottoms and the most bullish at or near market tops.

Chasing After the Hottest Issues

The largest losses in the stock market are often seen in the hottest issues, and many investors take excess risks in undiversified portfolios of such issues.

For example, many investors who loaded up on hot technology stocks during late 1998–1999, often on margin, incurred extreme losses as the NASDAQ Composite Index declined by more than 77% during the subsequent bear market.

This book offers some excellent strategies for assembling diversified portfolios of investments that are likely to outperform without involving the highest amount of risks. Greed is not necessarily good. Gain with a minimum of pain is very, very good.

Needing to Be in the Game All the Time

As they say among poker players, "there is a time to hold and a time to fold 'em."

Stocks show very nice rates of return about 50% of the time—definitely times to hold them.

Stocks show more indifferent rates of return about 30% of the time. You can probably hold some stronger industry groups or issues, but risks are generally too high to warrant remaining fully invested.

Stocks show losses about 20% of the time. Losses are not always severe, but risks can be very high. These are good periods to move into large or fully cash positions. You may miss the action, good or bad, but even if tracking the stock market is something you enjoy, wait until the market climate turns more positive.

And finally....

Needing to Be "Right" All the Time

Investors hate to "feel wrong" and love to "feel right."

As a result, many—probably most—market traders tend to sell profitable stocks too soon because it is fun to cash in profitable trades and to hold onto unprofitable stocks too long—and it is not fun to accept the fact that you have taken a loss (being "wrong"). Market traders often have problems selling stocks that have backed off from their highs because they feel that they cannot sell at a stock below a price that they might have secured in the past. ("I'll sell when it gets back to its best price.")

The fear of being wrong often blocks investors from taking any investment action at all.

You will learn totally objective stock market indicators that have had a history of producing profitable trades a high percentage of the time—not all the time, but a high percentage of the time.

If you follow these indicators, it does not mean that you have been "wrong" when losing trades do occur. You will have been right in· following an approach that provides favorable probabilities, but not perfection. Some losses are to be expected. It does not mean that your investment strategies have been wrong. It simply means that even the best strategies do not always produce perfect performance.

You will have committed no crime in following an objective strategy, even if some losses are taken. If you can overcome the fears of losing and the fears of being "out" of it, should the stock market rise unexpectedly, and simply follow the timing models you will be learning, then you are likely to perform very well over the long run.

CHAPTER 2

BOND-STOCK VALUATION MODELS— A KEY MARKET FORECASTING TOOL

Stock market analysts have expended countless hours—as well as countless dollars—in the quest for market forecasting tools and indicators, to predict the direction of stock prices.

However, indicators often contradict each other, or involve parameters that have to be modified at frequent intervals to reflect changes in market behavior. For example, it was believed during the 1970s that the stock market would be very likely to turn into a major bear market during times when average dividend payouts for stocks, represented in indices such as the Standard & Poor's 500 Index of major companies, declined to below 3.0%, or when price/earnings ratios (prices of shares divided by corporate profit per share) exceeded 20—that is, when investors had to pay $20 or more in share price for every $1 in earnings (profit) earned by companies.

In actuality, however, the stock market—if evaluated by these parameters—would have entered into a bear market by mid-1995, instead of rising to levels during 1999–2000 when shares were selling at approximately 46 times earnings, and dividend yields for the Standard & Poor's 500 Index were declining to approximately 1%.

The Search for Something Simple, Useful, and Stable

Both as an individual investor and as an investor of client capital, I (and my research staff) have been actively involved in the search for ideal stock market timing tools. In the process, I have developed many timing models of my own, and I have learned much from other students of the stock market, who have been good enough to share their knowledge with the public—including competitors such as myself.

I have come to a number of conclusions over the years.

Simple Is Better

For one, the simpler the market timing tool, the more likely it is to be successful. For various reasons, the more complicated the timing device, the less it is readily interpreted and the less it remains consistent in its performance.

Changes in Market Behavior Take Place

The stock market has changed its behavior in many ways over the years, perhaps as a result of large increases in trading volume, increased communication of information to the investing public, the greater computer power available for market analyses, and a higher level of investor sophistication. Market reactions to news events have become more immediate. Price movements that used to take days have become more intense and immediate. Market indicators have been modified again and again.

The task at hand is to identify useful stock market forecasting tools that have the ability to reliably, if not perfectly, identify those periods when stocks are relatively inexpensive, based upon their values compared to

other forms of investment (good times to buy), and when stocks are relatively expensive compared to other forms of investments, such as bonds (good times to maintain smaller percentages of assets in stocks).

If stocks are the best-valued form of investment around, that's where you want to put your money. If stocks are priced too high, risks increase, and your money is better placed elsewhere.

These relationships are the key to a set of excellent market timing indicators—indicators that are simple to maintain, that have functioned well (if not perfectly) for more than a quarter of a century, and whose premises are quite logical.

We recommend two variations of these indicators: the *Bond-Stock Valuation Models*.

Bond-Stock Valuation Models

Bond-Stock Valuation Models are indicators that, by comparing certain forms of return to investors from the bond and stock markets, provide a highly reliable gauge as to whether stocks or bonds represent the more favorable value for investors.

Historically, stocks have performed extremely well when earnings yields from stocks (covered later in the chapter) have compared favorably to interest returns available from government and medium-grade corporate bonds. Stocks have, historically, shown average performance during periods when bonds and stocks reflect equal value. On the other side, stocks have shown poor performance—losses on balance—when bonds have represented superior value. Investor capital moves from equities to investments that provide greater rates of return.

This class of indicator is probably most of what you need to know to successfully decide when and when not to accept risks inherent in investing in the stock market. However, as an added bonus, I will also provide an ancillary indicator, the "Weekly Breadth Model," which improves the performance of even the excellent Bond-Stock Valuation Models alone.

Consider some of the characteristics of the most useful stock market forecasting tools and then ask whether Bond-Stock Valuation Models meet the required criteria.

Desirable Qualities of Bond-Stock Valuation Models

Time Stability

In contrast to the indictors whose parameters have changed over the years, key indicators that I am recommending have functioned well in terms of their current parameters since 1981. This does not mean that the behavior of these indicators will necessarily be fixed for all time, but it does imply that as market-timing tools, they have been more stable than most.

Simplicity

The principles underlying this class of indicator are simple—no complicated mathematical prestidigitation are required.

Usefulness

Bullish zones are when most good things happen in the stock market. Prices rise in the most consistent way. Prices rarely decline seriously, and when they do decline for a few weeks—give or take—they tend to rebound quickly. More stocks tend to rise in price than to fall. Bullish zones are where most of the money is made in the stock market, and the least money is lost. These are the times when you should take your largest invested positions.

Neutral zones are periods when stocks show on average moderate gains, and sometimes serious losses. On balance, neutral zones produce favorable results for investors in the stock market, but not all that much more than money market funds. These are periods during which most investors should remove at least some capital from the stock market.

Bearish zones are when most bad things happen in the stock market. Prices tend to decline—sometimes seriously, sometimes moderately—and this is when your capital is likely to be better off in cash or in the safe haven of money market funds.

I will show you some excellent and efficient procedures by which you can determine whether bullish, neutral, or bearish conditions are in effect. In the process, we will review considerable past performance data, which will help you to maintain and to follow the direction of the indicators.

You will need to track only four readily available ingredients of your Bond-Stock Valuation timing models. These are defined next.

The Earnings Yield of the Standard & Poor's 500 Index

The *total annual earnings* of a corporation represent the *net profit* achieved each year from sales and other operations after costs and expenses are deducted. Growth companies employ profits for research, acquisitions, and expanded facilities and locations. Established, value-oriented companies are more inclined to provide dividend payouts to shareholders. Either way, shareholders benefit from high levels of earnings—either in the form of dividends or growth of corporate assets and market share or both.

The *price/earnings ratio* represents the amount of dollars in share value of the corporation required required by shareholders to receive one dollar of earnings. For example, suppose that Corporation XYZ shows a profit of $1 million and that the company has 500,000 shares outstanding. If we divide the $1 million profit by the 500,000 shares outstanding, there are $2 in earnings (or profit) for every share outstanding.

The question now is how much capital do shareholders have to invest in each share they own to secure $1 of corporate earnings? Suppose that the shares of Corporation XYZ trade at $50 per share. If you divide the price of each XYZ share, $50, by the amount of earnings per share, $2, the ratio of price to earnings is 25 ($50 price/$2 earnings per share). This is the price/earnings ratio.

Price/earnings ratios are considered to be significant by market analysts. Historically, shares of companies in the Standard & Poor's 500 have traded at an average price/earnings ratio of between 13 and 17, and in recent years, this is somewhat higher. As a general rule, the Standard & Poor's 500 is considered relatively expensive if investors have to pay more than $20 for each dollar of earnings, and relatively inexpensive below $13–$15, but there are other considerations involved. Corporations whose earnings are rising rapidly command higher price/earnings ratios than corporations with more stable earnings.

Where to Find Current Price/Earnings Ratios

Weekly data for the most recent 12-month price/earnings ratios for the Standard & Poor's 500 Index may be found in *Barron's Financial Weekly* in the "Market Laboratory" section, as well as in other financial publications.

Monthly readings can also be found on the Internet at http://www2.standardandpoors.com/spf/xls/index/sp500pe_ratio.xls.

Trailing Price/Earnings Ratios and Forward Price/Earnings Ratios

Market analysts report two variations of price/earnings ratios of stocks, as follows

- *Trailing ratios* refer to ratios calculated on corporate earnings already achieved. These ratios reflect the most recent twelve-month profits recorded and reported to the public.
- *Forward ratios* refer to calculations that employ current share price, coupled with assumptions of projected corporate earnings levels in the year ahead. Forward estimates often are overly optimistic, so forward price/earnings ratios tend to be lower than trailing ratios. Analysts who employ variations of the Bond-Stock Valuation Model tend to use forward price/earnings ratios in their calculations. I recommend the use of trailing or actual (already reported) earnings in the Bond-Stock Valuation market indicators.

There is one final calculation regarding the earnings component of Bond-Stock Valuation Models. This is the earnings yield, which is discussed next.

The Earnings Yield

Before examining the bond-related components of Bond-Stock Valuation Models, you need to make an additional calculation that enables you to make direct comparisons between returns from bond and stock investments.

The *earnings yield* relates earnings per share to share price in a manner that is comparable to the usual ways of stating rates of return from bond ownership.

For example, to find the current yield from a bond, divide the annual dollar payout of interest by the current price of the bond. For example, if a bond, selling at $1,000 (par), pays $50 per year in interest, its yield is 5% ($50 yield divided by $1,000 price = .05 or 5%).

If a stock earns $2 per year and has a price of $50 per share, divide 2 by 50 to secure the earnings yield, which is 4% (2 divided by 50 = .04 or 4%). This is simply the inverse of the price/earnings ratio, which is 25 in this example. A bond's current yield consists only of interest payments. A stock's current yield is the profit of the company, much of which may not directly accrue immediately to shareholders, but which does add to the value of their investment.

Investments to Be Compared

To Represent the Stock Market

Employ the 12-month trailing earnings yield of the Standard & Poor's 500 Index, which is readily available. *Barron's Financial Weekly* reports earnings yields and price/earnings ratios. For example, in the November 5, 2007 issue, in the "Market Laboratory" section, "Indices' P/Es and yields," the price/earnings ratio for the Standard & Poor's 500 Index was 17.80, and the earnings yield was 5.63%.

To Represent the Bond Markets

For the bond-stock comparison of income return and value, employ the yields of the Moody's average Baa quality (low investment grade) bond index to compare to the Standard & Poor's 500 Index earnings yield each week.

The rated investment-grade quality of these bonds (Baa) is the lowest investment grade (not speculative, but not the very highest quality), similar to the average quality ratings of stocks in the Standard & Poor's 500 Index. Because these bonds are lower grade than risk-free U.S. Government issues, their yields tend to be higher since investors do have to be rewarded for the extra risk the lower grade bonds involve.

The yield data for bonds is listed in *Barron's Financial Weekly*, in the "Market Laboratory" section, among other publications, and also at http://www.federalreserve.gov/releases/H15.

Look for the column headed by "week ending." Scroll down until you reach the weekly reading for Baa bonds. Weekly data works well—you will have to check just once each week. Historical data is also available at the site.

(For another bond-stock comparison, we will employ the average of yields of 90-day treasury bills and 10-year treasury notes. These reflect relationships between yields available from U.S. Government income instruments and yields of the Standard & Poor's 500 Index.)

The General Concept of Bond-Stock Valuation Models

The stock market tends to perform best when interest rates are declining or are expected to decline and tends to perform worst when interest rates are high and still rising.

Interest rates tend to decline when 1) economic activity is contracting, and there is less demand for loans; 2) there is low inflation; and 3) the Federal Reserve Board adjusts credit policy to make it easier for businesses to borrow in order to stimulate the economy. Bull markets often start during periods when the economy is still relatively weak, but when investors believe better days will come.

Interest rates tend to strongly rise during periods of economic expansion, which are also often marked by higher rates of inflation—borrowers have to pay more for credit. Savvy investors foresee slowdowns in the economy as a result of rising interest rates and sell stocks before the general public perceives the forthcoming change in trend.

It is often best to buy stocks following periods of economic weakness and sell when the economy has been favorable for many, many months. **Bear markets generally end and bull markets begin during periods when bad news prevails and the public and media are most pessimistic. Bull markets tend to end when good news prevails and the public and media are most optimistic.** Try to operate against the crowd when the crowd is nearly unanimous.

Lower interest rates encourage the economy, and higher interest rates discourage economic growth.

Money Goes Where It Is Best Treated

Flows of capital are most likely to move in the direction of the best reward, to places in which the money is best treated.

Stocks generally provide lower current income flows than bonds, which offer less opportunity for capital growth and, especially in the case of government bonds, are intrinsically safer. However, there are times when stocks, via their earnings yields, provide income returns competitive with bond yields, and sometimes even higher. When returns from stocks are high in comparison to bonds, investors are likely to place capital in stocks—the odds are very strong that stocks will then advance in price. When returns from stocks are low in comparison to bonds, investors are more likely to sell stocks and to move into bonds.

Bond-Stock Valuation Models define whether current relationships are bullish, neutral, or bearish for stocks.[1]

Interest Rate Relationships and Past Performance

Next, examine the relationships between bond interest and stock earnings yields and risk. For this, use the differences in return between Moody's average Baa bond yield and the trailing Standard & Poor's 500 Index earnings yield.

Figure 2.1 uses the upper and the lowest scales to show the relationships between Moody's Baa bond yields, the earnings yields of the Standard & Poor's 500 Index, and the price movement of the Standard & Poor's 500 Index.

1. A bond/stock model based upon the relationship of 10-year treasury bonds and forward-earning yields was originated in 1992 by Ed Yardini, an economist, and is known as the "Fed Model." My own variants of the Bond-Stock Valuation Model also draw from suggestions made by Ned Davis Research, Inc., a source of many useful market indicators and concepts.

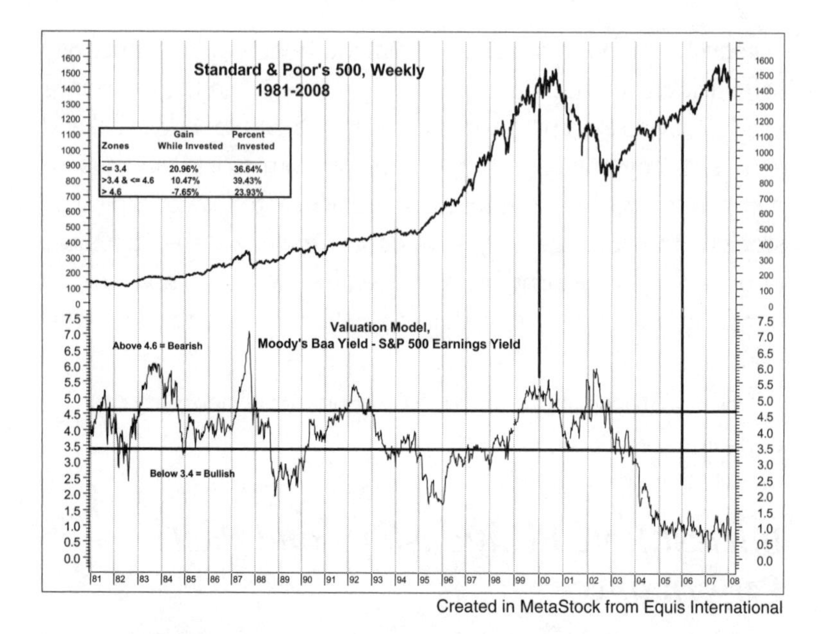

The chart shows the differentials between Moody's Average Baa bond yields and the earnings yields of the Standard & Poor's 500 Index, from 1981–2007. On October 30, 2007, the Baa bond yields were 6.39%; the S & P 500 earnings yield was 5.51%. The differential was only .88% (6.39% minus 5.51%), a bullish differential. (Source: Ned Davis Research, Inc.)

Figure 2.1
Spreads between Baa bond yields and Standard & Poor's 500 earnings yields

The lowest scale on the chart divides the differential into three sectors, discussed next.

Bearish Zones

The upper sector on the scale (differential greater than 4.6%) shows that bond yields are greater than stock earnings yields by a larger-than-average degree. This is a bearish implication for the stock market because capital receives above-average returns from bonds in comparison to stocks.

The bearish position of these differentials are notable during mid-1983, mid-1987, 1992, 1999, and early 2002—periods with either limited gains in the stock market or losses, at times severe. Such bearish periods have taken place 23.7% of the time. The Standard & Poor's 500 Index has had an average decline of 1.8% during these periods.

The stock market advances slightly more than 50% of the time, even while bearish signals are generated by the Baa Bond-Stock Valuation Model. However, gains, when they do occur, tend to be moderate. Losses, when they occur, have been more than 2½ times the size of gains. The Standard & Poor's 500 Index has reported average declines of 1.8% during periods when bearish signals are rendered.

Neutral Zones

The middle sector (differential between 3.4% and 4.6%) represents neutral periods. Although prices tend to rise during such periods, risks have been high.

Stocks have tended to advance during neutral periods of Baa Bond-Stock Valuation, at an average rate of 10.7% per year. However, some market declines have taken place while relationships have stood in this zone. The mid-zone of differentials between Baa bond yields and earnings yields of the Standard & Poor's 500 occurred 39.3% of the time. This is a somewhat bullish zone that has shown profitable results, as well as some losses over the years.

Bullish Zones

The lowest area of Figure 2.1 shows periods when the differentials between Baa bond yields and earnings yields of the Standard & Poor's 500 Index have been equal to or below 3.4%. These are the periods when stocks are priced at bargain levels in comparison to bonds. The best rates of return are from stocks at such times.

Stocks have performed well during periods when Baa bond yields were low in comparison to Standard & Poor's earnings yields. During these bullish periods, which occurred 37% of the time between 1981 and 2007, the New York Stock Exchange Index advanced at a rate of 20.4% per year. The same Index gained 9.6% per year, including all periods shown on the chart. **74.2% of this gain was recorded during the 37% of the time that the Baa bond yield – Standard & Poor's Index 500 earnings yield differential was most bullish.**

Baa bond yield—Standard & Poor's Index 500 earnings yield relationships remained bullish from 2003 to the end of 2007 (the time of this writing), supporting the advancing stock market. This model had correctly predicted more than four years of bull market profit with no serious declines.

If you had done nothing but invest only in the most bullish bond/stock periods, you would have been in the market only 37% of the time, but you would have secured 74.2% of the gains achieved by the Standard & Poor's 500 Index secured by buy-and-hold investors. At the worst, you would have incurred maximum loss from highest to lowest level of portfolio value of just 11.1%, occurring in August 2007. (Author's note: Drawdowns did briefly increase to above these levels during the first months of 2008, even as the favorable gap between Standard & Poor's Index 500 earnings, and yields of Baa bonds, became the greatest since the mid-1980s.)

Drawdown—loss between highest to lowest value—is a significant measure of market risk, and analysis of it should be considered in the formulations of your investment plan.

Maximum drawdown is the maximum loss that an investment incurs, or the true measure of risk. If an investment has lost 15% in the past, that is also possible in the future. A maximum drawdown of as little as 15%–17% is very low for ownership of stocks. Maximum historical drawdowns have been as high as 47% for the Standard & Poor's 500 Index and 77% for the NASDAQ Composite Index. Drawdown levels while the indicator was most bullish bolster the significance of the Baa Bond-Stock Valuation Model.

Table 2.1 further illustrates the Bond-Stock Valuation Model's ability to discriminate between favorable and unfavorable stock market periods.

TABLE 2.1
Comparisons of Baa Bond Yields/Standard & Poor's Index 500 Earnings and Stock Price Movement

	1981–2007 Comparisons Based on Performance of the New York Stock Exchange Index						
Bond Yield Minus S & P Yield	**Number of Periods**	**Profitable Periods**	**Avg. Gain**	**Unprofitable Periods**	**Avg. Loss**	**Avg. Result All Periods**	**Percent Invested**
Less than or equal to 3.4%	30	26 (86.7%)	+ 8.7%	4 (13.3%)	–2.1%	+7.26%	36.96%
Between 3.4% and 4.6%	51	29 (56.9%)	+ 6.9%	22 (43.1%)	–3.3%	+2.52%	39.31%
Greater than 4.6%	21	11(52.4%)	+ 2.7%	10 (47.6%)	–6.8%	-1.82%	23.72%

Note: These results are based on the assumption that traders enter and exit positions on the first trading days (usually Mondays) following the last trading days (usually Friday) of the previous week.

Note: Although the Baa Bond/Stock Indicator is based on relationships between yields of Baa bonds and earnings yields of the Standard & Poor's 500 Index, this example is based on the New York Stock Exchange Index. This is a weighted average of all stocks traded on the NYSE, representing a broader spectrum of stocks than the Standard & Poor's 500 Index and reflecting the performance of the average mutual fund.

Further Observations

There were 30 periods between 1981–2007 when the Baa Bond-Stock Valuation Model was most bullish.

Prices rose during 26 (86.7%) of those 30 periods, with gains averaging 8.71% per rising period. If you had been invested in the Standard & Poor's 500 Index during all periods when the indicator was favorably positioned, the odds were 9:1 that your investments would have been profitable.

Prices declined during four (13.3%) of 30 periods, with losses averaging 2.1% per losing period.

Further Evidence

The most bullish zones produced single-entry profits of 24.2% (1988–1990), 64.7% (1994–1997), 8.4% (1997–1998), and 65.5% (2003–2007). The best neutral zone profits were 21.7% (1982–1983), 55.8% (1985–1987), and 15.0% (1998–1999). The best single-entry gain during bearish periods was 12.5%, between 1983 and 1984.

There were no double-digit losses during the most bullish conditions from the beginning to the completion of trades, although there were double-digit interim drawdowns at times.

There were two double-digit losses during neutral periods: –13.5% from 1981–1982, and –11.8% in 1998.

Bearish periods produced the two single-largest losses between 1981 and 2007: –24.1% in 1987 and a loss of –20.0% during 2002.

It definitely pays to buy in the most bullish zone, to stay out of the most bearish zone, and to treat the neutral zone with caution.

Full trade-by-trade results appear in the appendix.

Chapter 3, "Government Bond Yields Compared to Earnings Yields," expands to a discussion of a second Bond-Stock Valuation Model and shows a way to improve results of either model by combining them into a Composite Bond-Stock Valuation Model.

CHAPTER 3

GOVERNMENT BOND YIELDS COMPARED TO EARNINGS YIELDS

Improving Results by Adding a Second Bond-Stock Valuation Model to Your Mix

In Chapter 2, "Bond-Stock Valuation Models—A Key Market Forecasting Tool," you examined the first of two Bond-Stock Valuation Models, which produced 27 years of positive results.

The bonds employed in the first Bond-Stock Valuation Model are the Baa corporate bonds, the lowest rank of investment-grade corporate bonds. The income instruments employed in the second model are the *safest* debt instruments in the United States—a combination of 90-day U.S. treasury bills, whose yields are averaged with the yields of 10-year U.S. Government Intermediate notes, both fully guaranteed by the U.S. Government.

Implications of the Safety of Government Instruments

As a general rule, the directions of interest rate movements among classes of debt instruments—Baa bonds, treasury bills, and 10-year U.S. Government notes—are concurrent. Interest payouts rise and fall in harmony. However, they sometimes diverge. For example, during periods of economic uncertainty, borderline-quality corporations may have to offer higher rates of interest to secure credit; yields of Baa bonds may also increase.

During periods of economic uncertainty, investors may want to move capital away from high risk to the most absolute safety available: United States Treasury-guaranteed debt instruments. When demand for these debt instruments increases, their prices rise in the open market. Because interest coupon rates are fixed, holders of government bonds benefit from increases in value. Although the amount of interest dollars they receive remains constant, their rate of return decreases. In addition, the U.S. government attracts investors to new bond issues with lower yields. So during periods of uncertainty, yields of government bonds frequently decline, while interest payout requirements of lower- or borderline-grade corporate bonds increase.

Ten-year treasury notes are considered safe if they are held until maturity, ten years from issue, at which time the debt is scheduled for full repayment. However, prices of these notes fluctuate during their life as prevailing interest rates change. Bond prices rise when prevailing interest rates decline. Bond prices decline when prevailing interest rates rise. To the extent that price fluctuations do occur over their life, ten-year treasury notes carry greater risk than treasury bills.

Averaging Yields of Longer-Term Treasury Notes and Shorter-Term Treasury Bills

The November 12, 2007, issue of *Barron's Financial Weekly* reported in the "Market Laboratory" section that 13-week

(90-day) treasury bills provided a coupon yield of 3.64%. On the same page, under "Adjustable Mortgage Base Rates," the yield for 10-year treasury notes was reported at 4.39%. By averaging 3.64% and 4.39, you can calculate the average yield: 4.015%.

Compare Earnings Yields from Stocks to Interest Yields, This Time from the Highest Grade of Government Income Issues

The first comparisons were between earnings yields of stocks and Baa corporate bonds. Stocks represent superior value to Baa bonds when those bonds provide a yield less than 3.4% greater than stocks. Baa bonds are better havens for capital when their yields rise to 4.6% above the yields of stocks.

Government debt instruments are higher quality than Baa bonds and do not have to pay as much interest to surpass the investment value of stocks.

Because 90-day treasury bills and 10-year treasury notes carry virtually no long-term risk, but stocks do carry risk, a portfolio of such debt instruments does not have to provide much income to be a superior investment.

Prospects are favorable for stocks when the earnings yield of the Standard & Poor's 500 Index is equal to or greater than 95% of the average of the government debt interest rate payouts (90-day treasury bill and the 10-year U.S. government note).

For example, the average interest payout of the government issues for the week ending November 12, 2007, was 4.015%. At that time, the price/earnings ratio of the Standard & Poor's 500 Index was 17.12. Its earnings yield was 5.84 percent

(1 divided by 17.12), well above 95% of the average yield (95% of 4.015% = 3.814%) of the government debt issues.

Stocks are in bullish position when the earnings yield of the Standard & Poor's 500 Index stands at 95%, or more than the average yield of 90-day treasury bills and 10-year U.S. government notes.

Neutral to Somewhat Bullish Zone

Prospects for the stock market are slightly better than neutral when the earnings yield of the Standard & Poor's 500 Index lies in the area between 85% and less than 95%.

For example, if the average yield of the government debt instruments was 4.015%, 85% of that yield is 3.413%. 94.99% of the average of the government debt instruments would be 3.814%. If the earnings yield of the Standard & Poor's 500 Index had been 3.413%–3.814%, the treasury interest based Bond-Stock Valuation Model would have been "neutral."

Implications of the Neutral to Moderately Bullish Zone

Stocks advance when the Bond-Stock Valuation Model is in this zone, but risks advance as well.

The Federal Bond-Stock Valuation Model is in a bearish zone when the earnings yield of the Standard & Poor's 500 Index stands below 85% of the average yield (of 90-day treasury bills and 10-year U.S. treasury notes).

For example, with the average government debt yield at 4.015% on November 12, 2007, the earnings yield of the Standard & Poor's 500 Index would have to be below 85% of that level (below 3.413%) to be bearish.

Figure 3.1 shows the relationship between the average yields of U.S. Government debt, the earnings yield of the Standard & Poor's 500 Index, and the price movement of the New York Stock Exchange Index.

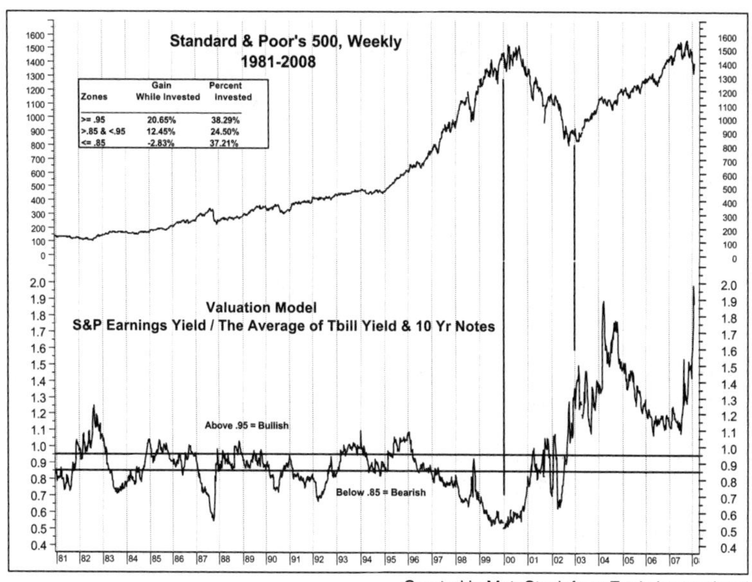

Created in MetaStock from Equis International

The stock market tends to perform well when earnings yields of the Standard & Poor's 500 Index stand above 95% of the average yield of 90-day treasury bills and 10-year U.S. government notes.

Figure 3.1
The price movement of the New York Stock Exchange Index coupled with yields of U.S. government debt instruments and the Standard & Poor's 500 Index earnings yield

Table 3.1 illustrates the relationships among bullish, neutral, and bearish configurations of government Bond-Stock Valuation levels and the movements of stock prices.

TABLE 3.1

Government Bond-Stock Valuation Relationships and Market Performance

Average Yields of 90-Day T-Bills and 10-Year U.S. Government Notes
Earnings Yield of the Standard & Poor's 500 Index
Market Index Employed, New York Stock Exchange Index

		1981–2007					
S & P Yield % of Bond Avg.	**Number of Periods**	**Profitable Periods**	**Avg. Gain**	**Unprofitable Periods**	**Avg. Loss**	**Avg. Result All Periods**	**Percent Invested**
≥ 95%	36	26 (72.2%)	+9.1%	10 (27.8%)	–1.2%	+6.30%	38.63%
85% to 95%	67	41 (61.2%)	+3.8%	26 (31.8%)	–2.4%	+1.40%	24.41%
≤ 85%	35	16 (45.7%)	+4.6%	19 (54.3%)	–5.0%	–0.57%	36.94%

Note: The Government Bond-Stock Valuation Model, in its most productive position, produced average annual gains of 6.2% while invested. This was 65.35% of the average annual gain (9.60%) of the NYSE Index while invested 38.6% of the time, which was an annualized rate of appreciation while invested 20.1% per year. During this period, the New York Stock Exchange Index appreciated at an annual rate of 9.61%.

Commentary

The discriminatory ability of this indicator captured 65.4% of the total annual stock market return, while invested only 38.6% of the time.

Those periods when the Government Bond-Stock Model showed stocks with their highest returns also produced the largest gains per stock market entry, the fewest and smallest losses, and the greatest consistency of successful market entries.

This model produced a winning batting average of 72.2% when favorably positioned. This is impressive enough but more impressive, perhaps, is the relationship between the average size of profitable entries (9.14%) compared to the average size of unprofitable entries (1.17%).

The odds on your side were greater than 20 to 1.

Taken altogether, 26 profitable entries produced a total gain of 237.64%, with the largest at 88.32%. Ten unprofitable entries produced a total loss of 11.7%, with the largest only 3.6%. The ratio of total gains to total losses, based on completed trades, was 20.3 to 1.

Handling Money Management at Other Times

The probabilities of profit have been very high during the 38% of the time when the U.S. Government Bond-Stock Valuation Model was in the most favorable zones. Stock market advances during those periods took place at rates of 20% per year.

Neutral to Moderately Bullish Zone

The neutral to moderately bullish zone for the U.S. Government Bond-Stock Valuation Model, which was found 24.4% of the time, produced annualized rates of return of 13.9%, better than a buy-and-hold strategy (9.61%). When the U.S. Government Bond-Stock Valuation Model was in a neutral to moderately profitable zone, percentage gains (157.0%) outnumbered percentage losses (62.9%), which is a ratio of 2.5 to 1.

The odds remain favorable for investors; however, gains per winning trade (average 3.8%) are limited, and the average trade showed a profit of just 1.4%. The probabilities justify stock positions when the Bond-Stock Valuation Model lies within this zone. Since 1981, the worst drawdowns were limited at 17.6%.

Conservative investors will want to take some capital off the table during periods that the U.S. Government Bond-Stock Valuation Model are no better than neutral, even if the odds of profitable stock trades remain positive.

The Negative Zone

The U.S. Government Bond-Stock Valuation Model has been in a negative zone 36.9% of the time since 1981, during which periods the stock market declined 1.15% per year. Although there have been periods when large gains took place in spite of negative indicator readings, the odds have not been with stocks during periods in which the indicator produces negative indications.

If you had based your investment decisions on the U.S. Government Bond-Stock Model alone, you would have been invested in stocks 63% of the time, and in cash 37% of the time.

The next chapter shows you how to vastly improve positive outcomes by creating a composite indicator using these bond-modeling systems.

CHAPTER 4

ACHIEVING A 92.59% PROFIT RATIO

Improving Returns with the Composite Bond-Stock Valuation Model

The two bond-stock valuation systems, the Baa Bond-Stock Valuation Model and the U.S. Government Bond-Stock Valuation Model, were previously explained. In this chapter, you first compare the performance of these two models. Then, by combining them, you produce a third model, which is superior to either alone.

Compare the reliability of the two models you have already examined in Tables 4.1, 4.2, and 4.3.

Table 4.1
1981–2007

Bullish Zone Performance

	Baa Bond-Stock Model	U.S. Government Bond-Stock Model
Percentage of time in bullish zone	36.96%	38.63%
Number of bullish zone entries	30	36
Profitable bullish zone entries	26 (86.7%)	26 (72.2%)
Average gain, profitable entries	+8.71%	+9.14%
Unprofitable bullish zone entries	4 (13.3%)	10 (27.8%)
Average loss, unprofitable entries	–2.1%	–1.2%
Annualized rate of return, all entries	**7.10%**	**7.35%**

Summary: Although the Baa Bond-Stock Model produced a higher percentage of winning entries in its most bullish zone, the U.S. Government Bond-Stock Model averaged higher percentage returns when in a favorable position, while losing less than the Baa Bond-Stock Model's unprofitable entries.

Table 4.2
Neutral to Moderately Bullish Zone Performance

	Baa Bond-Stock Model	U.S. Government Bond-Stock Model
Percentage of time in zone	39.31%	24.41%
Number of zone entries	51	67
Profitable entries into zone	29 (56.9%)	41 (61.2%)
Average gain, profitable entries	6.94%	3.8%
Unprofitable entries into zone	22 (43.1%)	26 (38.8%)
Average loss, unprofitable entries	–3.30%	–2.42%
Annual rate of return, all trades	**+2.5%**	**+ 1.4**

Summary: Investors participating in the stock market during neutral to moderately bullish zones for these models are better off employing the Baa Bond-Stock Valuation Model rather than the U.S. Government Bond-Stock Model. The Baa model produced higher annualized rates of return in this zone (+2.5% versus +1.4%), but did not trade as frequently as the U.S. Government Bond-Stock Valuation Model.

TABLE 4.3
Bearish Zone Performance

	Baa Bond-Stock Model	U.S. Government Bond-Stock Model
Percentage of time in zone	23.72%	36.94%
Number of zone entries	21	35
Profitable entries into zone	11	16
Average gain, profitable entries	2.65%	4.64%
Unprofitable entries into zone	10	19
Average loss, unprofitable entries	–6.81%	–4.96%
Annual rate of return, all trades	**–1.71%**	**–1.15%**

Summary: Although neither model produced net profits while in the bearish zone, the Baa Bond-Stock Valuation Model more clearly differentiated bearish periods from neutral periods, showing larger average losses during bearish periods, lower gains, and greater performance differentials between declining entries and rising entries. The Baa Bond-Stock Valuation Model isolates bearish periods better because it defines a smaller percentage of periods as bearish—23.7% of the time, as opposed to 36.9% of the time for the U.S. Government Bond-Stock Valuation Model.

And the winner is.... The Baa Bond-Stock Valuation Model is more efficient and accurate than the U.S. Government Bond-Stock Valuation Model.

Although the U.S Government Bond-Stock Valuation Model was more profitable in its most bullish zone, the Baa Model was more profitable when both the most bullish zone and the neutral to bullish zones were employed. It produced returns of 9.60% per year compared to 8.75% for the U.S. Government Model, requiring fewer round-trip transactions (56 versus 80). The fewer the trades, the lower the commission costs, the better.

The employment of government bonds in timing models is more widely known than the use of Baa bonds, an approach first brought to my attention by Ned Davis.

92.6% Reliability: Increasing Returns and Reducing Risk by Combining Your Two Bond-Stock Valuation Models

By using these models in combination, you can secure greater returns at lower risk than you can secure by using either model alone. The extra time and effort involved is minimal. The long-term rewards are considerable.

Review the bullish, neutral to bullish, and bearish parameters of both of the Bond-Stock Valuation Models described in Table 4.4.

TABLE 4.4
Rules of Bond-Stock Valuation Models

Baa Bond-Stock Valuation Model	U.S. Government Bond-Stock Model
Bullish: Baa bond yields less than 3.4% above S & P 500 trailing earnings yield.	**Bullish:** S & P 500 earnings yields are greater than 95% of the average of 90-day treasury bill yields and yield of 10-year treasury notes.
Neutral to Bullish: Baa bond yields between 3.4% and 4.6% above S & P 500 trailing earnings yield.	**Neutral to Bullish:** S & P 500 earnings yields lie between 85% and 95% of the average of 90-day treasury bill yields and yield of 10-year treasury notes.
Bearish: Baa bond yields are more than 4.6% above S & P 500 trailing earnings yield.	**Bearish:** S & P 500 earnings yields are less than 85% of the average of 90-day treasury bill yields and yield of 10-year treasury notes.

The Basic Principles of the Double-Entry Bond-Stock Valuation Timing Model

This timing model is designed to place investors into the stock market only when the odds are strongly favorable, when prospects for profits are far larger than prospects for losses.

There are only two conditions when this model places you or keeps you in the stock market:

- **Buy Condition #1:** You should remain invested in the stock market if BOTH the Baa Bond-Stock Valuation Model and the U.S. Government Bond-Stock Model lie within their most bullish zones.
- **Buy Condition #2:** You should remain invested in the stock market if EITHER the Baa Bond-Stock Valuation Model OR the U.S. Government Bond-Stock Model lie within their most bullish zones.

For condition #1 to be met, Baa bonds must provide yields no greater than 3.4% above the earnings yield of the Standard & Poor's 500 Index, and the earnings yield of the Standard & Poor's 500 Index must be at least 95% of the average yield of the 90-day treasury bill and the 10-year treasury note.

As an illustration, if the price/earnings ratio of the Standard & Poor's 500 Index is at 17, its earnings yield (1 divided by 17) is 5.88%. If Baa bonds were paying 8.0% interest, the Baa yield (8.0%) would be only 2.12% greater (8.0% minus 5.88%) than the S & P 500 earnings yield; this puts the Baa Bond-Stock Valuation Model in its most favorable zone. If the 90-day treasury bill is yielding 4.1%, and the 10-year U.S. Government note is yielding 4.4%, the average yield of the two is 4.25%. With the S & P 500 earnings yield at 5.88%, it is above 95% of that average. With both elements present, a Condition #1 buy signal is in effect.

A summary of the historical performance of Condition #1 entries into the stock market is shown in Table 4.5. As you can see condition #1 buy signals are reliable and profitable, and carry a high degree of safety.

Condition #2 is met when either model (but not both) lies within its most favorable bullish zones. This occurs if Baa bond yields are not greater than 3.4% above the level of the trailing earnings yield of the Standard & Poor's 500 Index, or if the earnings yields of the Standard & Poor's 500 Index are at least 95% of the average of yields of the 90-day treasury bills and the 10-year U.S. Government notes. If both qualifications are met, a Condition #1 configuration is in place, which carries more favorable implications.

If you simply remember to invest in stocks when both—or even just one—of your Bond-Stock Valuation Models lie in favorable position, your investment portfolio is likely to prove to be profitable.

Table 4.5
Performance Results While in Buy Zones of Condition #1 and of Condition #2 Based upon the NYSE Index, 1981–2007

Condition #1								
Percent of Time Invested	# of Entries	# of Winning Entries	Avg. % Gain	# of Losing Entries	Avg. % Loss	Avg. +/- All Entries	Rate of Return While Invested	Max. Draw-down
24.85%	27	25 (92.6%)	6.00%	2 (7.4%)	2.83%	+ 5.35%	20.84%	–11.9%

Summary

25 of 27 entries (92.6%) were profitable, for a total percentage gain of 150.02%. Total percentage losses during two losing entries were 5.66%. The ratio of total winning to losing percentages was 26.5:1. For each 1% loss, entries based on Condition #1 parameters earned 26.5%. Compound annual gains during periods that Condition #1 were in effect produced an annual return of 4.82% per year while invested only 24.85% of the time. The NYSE Index, which advanced at an average rate of 9.61% per annum, rose at a rate of 20.84% per annum during times when Condition #1 was in effect.

These preceding results reflect time frames when Condition #1 was in effect, and do not include the entire time that invested positions might have been open.

Condition #2

Table 4.6 shows the performance of the NYSE Index from 1981–2007, when only one of the two valuation models was at the most bullish position. "Entries in" may occur as a result of one Bond-Stock Valuation Model moving from "neutral" to bullish, while the other remained in neutral. "Entries in" may also have occurred when one bond-valuation deteriorated from bullish to neutral, while the other remained bullish. Similarly, "exits out" may have occurred when both models rose to bullish zones from a condition when only one was bullish while the other was neutral. This may have resulted from a model falling from bullish to neutral, whereas prior to the exit, one model was neutral while the other was bullish.

TABLE 4.6

Percent of Time Invested	# of Entries	# of Winning Entries	Avg. % Gain	# of Losing Entries	Avg. % Loss	Avg. +/- All Entries	Rate of Return While Invested	Max. Draw-down
25.89%	61	35 (57.4%)	5.15%	26 (42.6%)	–1.84%	+2.17%	+19.18%	–16.8%

Condition #1 (24.85%) and Condition #2 (25.89%) occurred with almost equal frequency. The annualized rates of return (+19.18%), while invested during periods that Condition #2 was in effect were slightly below the annualized rates of return (20.84%), achieved when Condition #1 periods were in effect. Risk was higher during Condition #2 periods, with –16.8% maximum drawdown, whereas Condition #1 showed maximum drawdowns of only –11.9%. The profit reliability of Condition #2 periods fell short of the profit reliability of Condition #1 periods—57.4% (#2) versus 92.6% (#1).

Blended Performance (1981–2007)

Table 4.7 is a blend of entries based on Conditions #1 and #2, and represents the performance of accounts, presuming they were fully invested when either Condition #1 or Condition #2 buy signals, or both, were in effect, but not at other times. There was no income credit allowance for the periods when stocks were not held, which was approximately half the time.

28 of 39 entries (71.8%) proved profitable, for an average gain per entry of 7.8%. The rate of return while invested was 19.99% per year, which was more than twice the rate of return of buy-and-hold strategies. The annualized rates of return as a result of being invested in the New York Stock Exchange Index only in favorable bond-stock valuation periods was 9.69%, which was slightly better than the rate of gain, 9.61% annualized, shown over the years for the New York Stock Exchange Index on a buy-and-hold basis. In this comparison, your portfolio would have been subject to risk only about 50% of the time, incurring only one-third the maximum losses taken by the New York Stock Exchange Index. These comparisons, again, do not include the benefits of interest earned while in cash positions.

Table 4.7
Combined Performance, Condition #1, and Condition #2 Entries

Percent of Time Invested	# of Entries	# of Winning Entries	Avg. % Gain	# of Losing Entries	Avg. % Loss	Avg. +/- All Entries	Rate of Return While Invested	Max. Draw-down
50.74%	39	28 (71.8%)	11.17%	11 (28.2%)	1.21%	+7.68%	19.99%	−16.71%

Your investment strategy would involve maintaining high percentages of assets in stocks when at least one of the Bond-Stock Valuation Models was within its bullish zone. Higher percentages would be invested when both Bond-Stock Valuations Models were within their bullish zones. Even higher levels of stock holdings would be maintained when "Weekly Breadth Signals" were in effect. This is covered in coming pages.

Periods with Lower Profit Potential

The idea behind successful investing is NOT to be invested at all times, but to be invested only during those times most likely to show profits and least likely to produce losses. One subset of market conditions—comprising 50% of the time—keep the odds heavily in favor of stocks. These times reflect above-average rates of return (19.99% rate of return while invested, compared to 9.61% for all periods) and much lower drawdowns.

Consider two additional potential investment periods. The first is a more neutral period, when at least one of the Bond-Stock Valuation Models stands in neutral territory but neither stands in its most bullish area as shown in Table 4.8. The second is a bearish period when *both* bond-stock models stand in negative territory.

In this neutral zone, both valuation models lie in the neutral zone, or one but not both lie in the bearish zone.

However, neither lies in the most bullish zone.

TABLE 4.8
Condition #3—At Least One Bond Valuation Model Lies in Neutral Territory, but Neither Is in Its Most Bullish Zone

Percent of Time Invested	# of Entries	# of Winning Entries	Avg. % Gain	# of Losing Entries	Avg. % Loss	Avg. +/- All Entries	Annualized Rate of Return While Invested	Max. Draw-down
29.09%	58	33 (56.9%)	4.12%	25 (43.10%)	3.09%	+1.10%	7.25%	–29.5%

The stock market advances during periods when both the Baa Bond-Stock Valuation and the U.S. Government Bond-Stock Valuation Model remain in neutral territory. Rates of return exceed the general rates of return available from risk-free investments, such as money market funds. However, risks are high—a maximum drawdown of as much as 29% taking place at times between 1981–2007. These are not the best times to aggressively invest in stocks.

A Signal to Stay Absolutely Clear of the Stock Market

Avoid stocks when both Bond-Stock Valuation Models lie within their most negative zones—a condition that has taken place 20% of the time since 1981. The largest gain during such periods was 6.25% (1991–1992). However, closed-out losses of more than 25% have occurred, with interim losses exceeding 44% at times (see Table 4.9). The rate of loss during periods when both Bond-Stock Valuation Models were negative averaged more than 2.1% per year since 1981. Annualized, the rate of return during bearish periods was –12.1%.

TABLE 4.9
Condition #4—Both Bond-Stock Valuation Models Are in Bearish Territory

Percent of Time Invested	# of Entries	# of Winning Entries	Avg. % Gain	# of Losing Entries	Avg. % Loss	Avg. +/- All Entries	Annualized Rate of Return While Invested	Max. Draw-down
20.15%	21	10 (47.62%)	1.95%	11 (52.38%)	–6.43%	–2.44%	–10.19%	–44.24%

Summary

Adopt the following procedures:

1. Learn and maintain the procedures and data to track two Bond-Stock Valuation Models: the Baa Bond-Stock Valuation Model and the U.S. Government Bond-Stock Valuation Model.
2. Maintain the largest stock positions during periods when both valuation models are in their most favorable zones (best) or during periods when at least one of the two models are within their favorable zone. Between these two conditions, expect to be invested approximately 50% of the time.
3. Periods when neither model reside within their most bullish zone, but are neutral, are likely to be somewhat profitable for stocks, but with high levels of risk. Aggressive investors may retain some stock positions during such times. Conservative investors may prefer to remain partially or fully in cash position.
4. Stocks should be avoided during the roughly 20% of the time that both bond-stock valuations are in their most bearish zones. These are periods when the odds do not favor the stock market.

A very different class of stock market indicator employs the behavior of the stock market to identify stronger-than-average market prospects. This indicator, used in conjunction with the Bond-Stock Valuation Models, increases your profit edge over the random investor, producing greater returns than the bond-stock valuation indicators while incurring no significant additional risk. That is the topic of the next chapter.

CHAPTER 5

HOW TO GAUGE THE TRUE INNER PULSE OF THE STOCK MARKET

Including a Special Indicator Whose Buy Signals Have Proven Profitable More Than 81% of the Time Over the Past Quarter Century

In this chapter, you learn about a stock market indicator that requires only a few minutes each week to maintain and to calculate, and that has had an exemplary record of performance since 1981 (and earlier). This indicator improves the already excellent performance of the Twin Bond-Stock Valuation Model by recognizing and expanding the favorable periods during which you might want to be invested.

You will need to spend just a few minutes each week, evaluating certain readily available data, to maintain this tool. Before we move into further particulars, let's consider a measure of market stock performance that, in many ways, is more significant than changes in the well-known Dow Industrial Average.

The Significance of Breadth in the Stock Market

Most media reports of stock market activity each day include references to price changes in the levels of various market indices, each of which largely represents a certain segment of the stock market. The Dow Industrial Average, approximately one-century old at this time, is probably the best known—although the 30 stocks that comprise this index now represent less than 1% of the nearly 3,600 issues (as of December 2007) that trade on the New York Stock Exchange, not to mention the greater number of issues that trade elsewhere. The Standard & Poor's 500 Index is the most frequently employed benchmark of market performance—more broad in its composition than the Dow, but includes, still, only a fraction of the number of issues traded.

Moreover, both of these market indices are weighted to reflect the relative size of the corporations included, so, in both cases, larger companies exert a greater influence upon the level of the index than smaller companies. Most other indices are similarly weighted—the NASDAQ Composite Index is heavily influenced by larger companies such as Microsoft and Intel.

As much as these indices include relatively few issues, and are weighted so that the largest companies exert the largest influence, they do not always reflect the strength or weakness of the average stock or the performance of the entire stock market. For this, knowledgeable investors often employ more broadly based market indices. These include, for example, the Value Line Composite Index, which provides equal weight to all of its component issues, or indicators such as advance-decline differentials, which represent the differences between the number of stocks that advance and the number that decline each day (or week).

Advance-Decline Indicators

Advance-decline data reflect the "breadth" of the stock market, which means the numbers of stocks that advance in price each day (or week) and the numbers that decline in price. The ratio of stocks that advance each day (advancing issues) and stocks that decline in price (declining issues) provide significant information regarding the relative percentages of stocks that are actually participating in advances or declines (readings of market breadth) that take place in the stock market.

During truly strong market periods, gains in indices such as the Dow Industrials and the Standard & Poor's 500 Index should be confirmed by strong readings in market breadth. There should be many more issues advancing than declining to confirm large gains in market indices like the Dow. Such breadth confirmations are usually signs of broad, underlying strength in the general stock market, and imply further gains to come. Weakening market breadth readings—even if major market indices continue to advance—imply a narrowing of strength in the stock market, which is often a precursor of more apparent weakness to come, and a reduction in the likelihood of ongoing gain for stocks.

For example, although speculative interest drove the prices of technology stocks to new heights during 1999 and early 2000, market breadth was actually generally weak during this period; a bear market starting for a large proportion of issues under cover of a strong rally in relatively few market sectors. This weakening of market breadth was a precursor to the general and severe bear market that developed in March 2000. Conversely, the market advance that started in March 2003 was broad and general, signifying the confirmation of a new major bull market. Figure 5.1 shows the cumulative weekly net differentials between the numbers of issues advancing and declining on the New York Stock Exchange, 2000–2008, a period during which stocks rising in price generally outnumbered stocks that were declining in price.

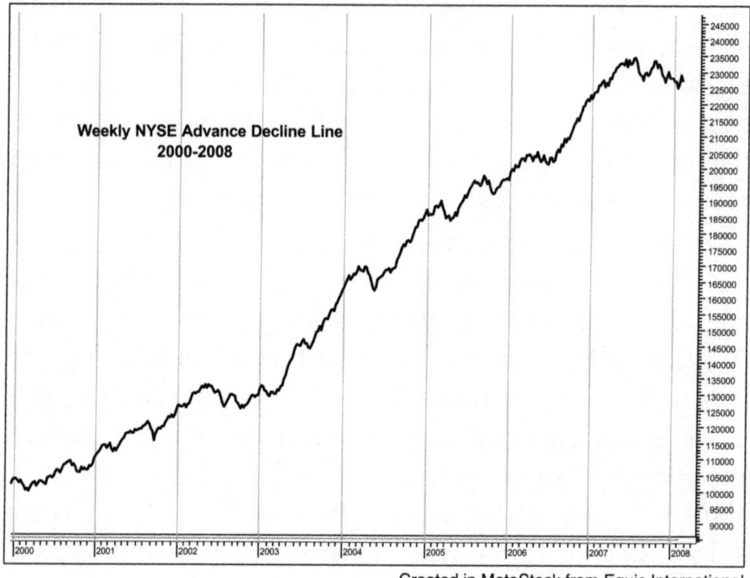

This chart shows the cumulative net difference between advancing and declining issues on the New York Stock Exchange, based upon weekly closing prices. Market breadth has tended to retain strength over the years.

Figure 5.1
Cumulative weekly advance-decline line and New York Stock Exchange Index (2000–2008).

For further information and other charts relating to the advance-decline line, do a search of the web relating to "advance-decline line." A number of interesting and informative articles will appear.

There is a very useful indicator that measures the relative strength of the advancing segment of the stock market, compared to the declining segment of the stock market; it is based usually on daily or weekly ratios of the number of stocks that advance on the New York Stock Exchange and the number that decline. As a general rule, the stock market is likely to perform well during periods in which the numbers of stocks that advance in price exceed numbers that decline.

For our purposes, we will be particularly interested in those relatively few occasions during which a special breadth indicator identifies far above-average favorable market breadth by identifying unusually positive relationships between stocks that advance in price and those that decline—or to put it another way, when advances outnumber declines by very large, specified amounts over periods of a number of weeks. We will refer to these unusually powerful surges in market breadth as *Breadth Signals*.

In the past, these signals have proven to be excellent foretellers of further gains in the stock market, with such gains taking place in addition to gains already achieved prior to the generation of breadth confirmations of market strength. It has generally paid to initiate additional stock positions at times that these signals are generated and to hold existing positions until there is evidence that market breadth is weakening. This evidence, when it does develop, cancels the bullish implications of the breadth confirmation signals in effect.

You will see the past performance of Breadth Signals for the 1970–2007 period, and will be able to evaluate its worth yourself. Let's review the data required and methods of calculation involved.

Required Data to Calculate Breadth Signals

The first step in this process is to calculate the *Weekly Breadth Reading*.

Only three items of data are required, which are posted on weekends or on Mondays to reflect the week just completed. These items are as follows:

- The number of issues on the New York Stock Exchange that have advanced in price during the week just completed.
- The number of issues on the New York Stock Exchange that have declined in price during the week just completed.
- The total number of issues traded each week on the New York Stock Exchange, including advancing issues, declining issues, and issues that are unchanged in price.

This data is available in *Barron's Financial Weekly*—which is published on weekends, and dated the following Mondays—in the "Market Laboratory" section, next to the charts, in a section called "Market Advance/Decline Totals." Make sure you record the weekly composite data, and not any of the daily data that are also presented on the same page.

Because *Barron's* also carries the bond and earnings data required to compare bond interest payouts with the earnings yields of the Standard & Poor's 500 Index, you might find it worthwhile to subscribe to either the delivered or online versions of the newspaper.

The Calculations Required for the Weekly Breadth Reading

The October 29, 2007, issue of *Barron's Financial Weekly* reported, in its Trading Diary on the "Market Laboratory" page, that during the week ending October 26, the following took place on the New York Stock Exchange:

Number of Issues Traded	3,578
Advancing Issues	2,277
Declining Issues	1,234

Using this data, we make the following calculation:

Weekly Breadth Reading = (number advancing issues – number declining issues) divided by the total number of issues traded

or

(2,277 – 1,234) divided by 3,578

or

1043 divided by 3,578, which equals 0.2915 or 29.15%

To state this calculation another way, see the following table:

A	B	C	D	E
Number of Advancing Issues	Number of Declining Issues	Advancing minus Declining Issues (Column A – Column B)	Total Number of Issues Traded	Column C divided by Column D = *Weekly Breadth Reading*
2277	1234	1043	3578	1043 / 3578 = .2915

We will refer to the final calculated result (.2915) as the Weekly Breadth Reading.

The preceding calculation represented a strong week for the stock market—nearly twice as many issues advanced in price as declined. There were strong price gains in the various market indices as well. The Dow Industrials advanced by 2.1%, the Standard & Poor's 500 Index by 2.3%, and the NASDAQ Composite Index by 2.9%, so strength appeared in market breadth readings, as well as in the market indices, which are most influenced by larger companies.

Another Example

Here is another example of calculating the Weekly Breadth Reading:

> (Number of advancing issues – number of declining issues on the New York Stock Exchange) divided by the total number of issues traded on the New York Stock Exchange

During a given week, there are 2,000 issues on the New York Stock Exchange that have risen in price. On that same week, there are 1,500 issues on the New York Stock Exchange that have declined in price. During that week, 3,700 issues have traded. This amount will be greater than the sum of advancing + declining issues because a certain number of issues remain unchanged in price each week.

The formula for weekly breadth readings would be as follows:

$$\frac{2000 \text{ (rising issues)} - 1500 \text{ (declining issues)}}{3700 \text{ total issues} = 3700} = \frac{500}{3700} = \mathbf{.135}$$

If there were 1,500 advancing issues and 2,000 declining issues, then the calculation would be as follows:

$$\frac{1500 \text{ (rising issues)} - 2000 \text{ (declining issues)}}{3700 \text{ total issues} = 3700} = \frac{-500}{3700} = \mathbf{-.135}$$

The highlighted final ratios (+/–.135) are significant numbers. These numbers reflect the extent to which market breadth is favorable—ratios of gaining to losing stocks as a proportion of the total market (positive, negative, and how positive or negative).

The Next Step—Creating a Six-Week Exponential Moving Average of Weekly Readings

Please do not let that fancy term, "exponential moving average," disturb you.

Once you get the idea, you will see how much time exponential averages can save you.

Moving Averages

Moving averages are averages of the latest stock market daily, weekly, or monthly closings and such that are maintained to provide smoother representations of market data. For example, let's suppose that you want to maintain a five-week average of the following data stream: 3, 7, 15, 8, 5. Each number reflects one weekly closing reading. The five-week average level of this data is equal to the five-week sum of each week's level divided by 5, or 38/5 = 7.60.

Let's suppose that a sixth week shows a weekly reading of 12. Because you are calculating five-week averages, based on the most recent five-week data points, you drop the furthest back reading, 3; adding the new weekly reading to the total that will again be divided by 5. (You now add 7, 15, 8, 5, and 12 to secure a five-week total of 47.) This new five-week total of weekly entries, 47, is now divided once again by 5 to secure an updated five-week moving average, 9.40. This form of moving average is considered to be a "simple or basic moving average."

Figure 5.2 illustrates a stream of stock prices with a 21-week moving average. You can see how the average smoothes weekly entries to reflect the direction and strength of longer-term market trends. In this form of moving average, all the data points within that average receive equal weight.

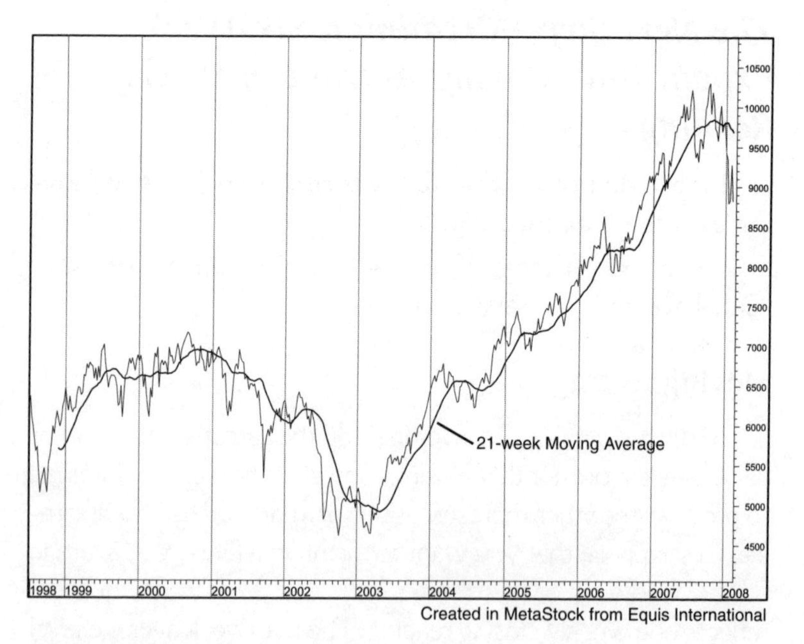

The 21-week moving average of the New York Stock Exchange Index represents the significant trend of that index. Notice how it tracked the bear market, 2000–2002, and then the bull market, 2003–2006.

Figure 5.2

New York Stock Exchange Index 21-week moving average (2000–2006).

Exponential Moving Averages

The *exponential moving average (EMA)* is a means of smoothing data that places greater weight upon recent data than past data; it is therefore more sensitive to recent price movement than simple moving averages that reflect the same time span.

Exponential moving averages are not maintained in the same manner as straight moving averages, described previously. The procedures are actually quite different. At first, the differences may appear daunting, but once you grasp the procedures involved, you will find exponential averages to actually be quite simple to maintain and follow.

Why Not Simply Use Regular Moving Averages?

In certain applications, exponential moving averages appear to provide more efficient signals than straight moving averages, in good part because they are more influenced by recent data than past data and are, therefore, more quickly responsive to changes in trend than regular moving averages. Our research, dating back to 1970, indicates that Weekly Breadth Readings are considerably more accurate when they are based upon exponential moving averages than when they are based on straight moving averages.

You may find the next few pages to be difficult, particularly if you are not mathematically inclined. Please take my word, however: **The effort is very likely to prove worthwhile!** Breadth Signals have proven to be highly reliable and powerful for decades.

If all else fails, you can simply employ only the comparisons between bond and stock returns to investors that you have already learned for the assessment of market conditions.

However, Weekly Breadth Readings, using exponential moving averages, will add to the benefits of these comparisons. Give yourself an extra benefit. Stay the course until you fully understand the procedures I will be showing you.

The First Step in Maintaining Exponential Averages: The Smoothing Constant

The first step in maintaining an exponential average is the determination of the *smoothing constant*. This is done by dividing the number of weeks you want to include in your weekly exponential moving average (N), plus 1, into the number, 2. Because you are looking for a six-week exponential average in your maintenance of the Weekly Breadth Readings, you divide N + 1 (or in this case, 6 + 1) into 2 to secure the result, .286 (2 divided by 7); this becomes the smoothing constant that we shall employ.

The Formula for Calculating an Exponential Moving Average (EMA)

To calculate each week's new six-period exponential moving average, you always need the previous week's exponential moving average as a basic part of the calculation. However, when you first create an exponential average of a stream of data, you need to have someplace to start, and you will NOT have an exponential average to begin with. Therefore, although they are not quite the same thing, the initial data point may be established by employing a six-week *simple* moving average in lieu of the exponential average.

You will be using a simple moving average in this manner only once, when you are calculating an initial average to begin the process. Thereafter, you will have exponential averages available to you to carry through the full formula.

For the purpose of explaining the process, in the next example, we will be using the price of a stock as our data point, not the Weekly Breadth Reading, which is our ultimate goal.

To perform the calculation process for the first time, you will need the following three things:

- The six-week exponential smoothing constant we have calculated as .286.
- Last week's six-week simple moving average of whatever data you are using; for the purposes of this example, let's say this is the price of a stock, and that the six-week simple moving average has been determined to be 55.
- This week's new data point or price, which we will say is $60. Note that the new data point is not an average, but is the actual current price of the stock.

With these three pieces of data, the initial calculation is expressed in the following steps:

1. Multiply .286 times this week's actual price, or $60, minus the previous week's six-week simple moving average, or 55. In other words, multiply .286 times 5 ($60 minus 55), which equals 1.43.
2. Add *back* the previous week's moving average of 55, to 1.43, which equals 56.43.
3. 56.43 is the new six-week exponential moving average.

That's it.

Now, from this point forward, you will no longer use the six-week *simple* moving average as a starting point, because you now have calculated your first six-week exponential moving average (EMA) as 56.43.

So, let's say that a week has gone by, and you are ready to calculate the new six-week exponential moving average for the current week. Let's also say that the new price point of the stock is now $61.

Using the six-week exponential moving average, the calculation can be expressed as follows:

> .286 × (this week's data point of $61 – last week's exponential moving average of 56.43 = 4.57) + last week's exponential moving average of 56.43 = the new six-week exponential average.
>
> (.286 × 4.57 = 1.30), plus 56.43 = 57.73
>
> So, 57.73 is the new six-week exponential moving average (EMA).

This is neither difficult, nor very time consuming, once you know how to do it.

Note that in each calculation, you are using the previous week's EMA *twice*: the first time to subtract it and the second time to add it. Explaining why this is necessary, or why it works, is not the mission of this book. Suffice it to say it does work, and will help you be much more successful as an investor.

Before you learn how to apply the exponential moving average to the Weekly Breadth Readings, you might find it helpful to review the following examples of how to calculate the exponential moving average, using stock prices again as the basic data.

Applying the Formula: First Example

Suppose that last week you calculated the six-week EMA of a stock price as 50. This week, the stock closed at 57. Given this information, here is how you would calculate this week's exponential moving average of the stock price:

$$.286\ (57 - 50) + 50 = (.286 \times 7) + 50 = 2.002 + 50 = 52.002.$$

Latest Price = 57 | Prior Week's Exponential moving Average = 50 | This Week's Exponential Average

Now suppose that the following week, the stock declines to 38. In that case, you update the six-week exponential moving average of the stock price as follows:

$$.286\ (38 - 52) + 52 = (.286 \times -14) + 52 =$$
$$= 4.004 + 52 = 47.996$$

New Price = 38 | Prior Week's Exponential Moving Average = 52 | Most Recent Weekly Exponential Moving Average

Handling Negative Numbers

Negative numbers are numbers whose values are below zero (0). For example, if a person has $10,000 in assets but owes $15,000 in debt, his net assets come to –$5,000—a negative number, reflecting a value below 0.

In the second example, the calculation involved the multiplication by a positive number of a negative number (.286 × –14), and the addition of a negative number (–4.004) to a positive number (52).

(Further discussion regarding the handling of calculations that include negative as well as positive numbers, as well as useful Internet resources relating to these processes, appears in the appendix.)

In some of your weekly calculations, you might encounter the need to deal with both positive and negative numbers. After you become familiar with the procedures involved, you will handle everything with ease.

At this point in the chapter, you have learned how to calculate two things:

- The Weekly Breadth Reading
- An exponential moving average

Now it is time to learn how to combine them to calculate the important Breadth Signal mentioned earlier.

Calculating the Exponential Moving Average of the Weekly Breadth Reading

The example that follows essentially replicates a similar example, discussed previously. However, because the concepts involved are significant, the repetition seems worthwhile:

Step 1: At the end of each week, calculate the Weekly Breadth Reading: Subtract the number of issues on the New York Stock Exchange that declined in price from the number that advanced during the week.

For example, if there were 1,500 advancing issues and 1,000 declining issues, the Breadth Reading would be +500, a positive number. If there were 1,000 advancing issues and 1,500 declining issues, the Breadth Reading would come to –500, a negative number.

Step 2: Divide the result of Step 1 by the number of total issues traded, which include issues that are unchanged in price. The result is **a weekly ratio of the differential between the number of advancing minus declining**

issues each week ("Weekly Breadth Reading") and the total number of issues traded each week.

For example, if the net breadth reading is +500, and if the total number of issues traded that week is 3,000, the weekly ratio of net breadth divided by the total number of issues traded would come to 500/3000 or to .167.

If the breadth reading were to be –500, and if the total number of issues traded that week is 3,000, then the weekly breadth reading would come to –500/3000 or to –.167.

For the purpose of maintaining the all-important Breadth Signals, you now have to calculate, each week, a six-week exponential moving average of Weekly Breadth Readings. Use the following formula (keep in mind that translating this process into words makes it sound much more complicated than it really is):

.286 × (this week's Weekly Breadth Reading – last week's six-week exponential average (EMA) of the Weekly Breadth Reading) + last week's six-week EMA of the Weekly Breadth Reading = the new EMA of Weekly Breadth Reading

This can be shortened to read:

.286 × (this week's Weekly Breadth Reading – last week's EMA) + last week's EMA = the new EMA of Weekly Breadth Reading

This is the same formula that we employed in the previous examples using the price of a stock. However, this time we are calculating six-week exponential averages of the Weekly Breadth Readings.

Example

Let's say that last week's six-week exponential moving average (EMA) of the Weekly Breadth Reading was .10 or 10%.

This week, there were 2,000 rising issues and 1,500 declining issues, making a positive net differential of +500 in market breadth. 3,700 issues were traded during the week.

The Weekly Breadth Reading this week came to +.135 because (2000 – 1500) divided by 3700 = 500/3700 = +.135.

The new six-week exponential moving average = .286 (.135 – .10) + .10.

= .286(.035) + .10.

= .0100 + .10

= .110 (the new six-week exponential moving average of the Weekly Breadth Reading)

In this case, there were more advancing than declining issues for the week. If there had been more declining than advancing issues, you would have had to deal with negative numbers.

Further examples, this time from real historical data, follow next.

The following examples represent actual weekly advance-decline data on the New York Stock Exchange, between the weeks ending October 26, 2007 and November 9, 2007, as reported in *Barron's Financial Weekly*. The data used in the examples can be found in Table 5.1.

TABLE 5.1
Calculation of Six-Week Exponential Moving Averages of Weekly Impulse Ratio Levels, October–November 2007

	A	B	C	D	E	F
Date	**Number of Advances**	**Number of Declines**	**Net Advances minus Declines (Column A minus Column B)**	**Total Number of Issues**	**Weekly Breadth Readings (Column C divided by Column D)**	**The Six-Week (.286) Exponential Average of Column E**
10/26/07	2,277	1,234	+1043	3,578	.2915	.053 (note A)
11/2/07	1,179	2,350	–1171	3,588	–.3264 (note B)	–.056 (note C)
11/09/07	670	2,870	–2200	3,577	–.6150 (note D)	–.215 (note E)

Notes from Table 5.1

A: You could not calculate this exponential average using only the data in Table 5.1 because doing so would require data from previous weeks that is not shown here. If you had been keeping track of the Weekly Breadth Readings during the weeks prior to 10/26/07, you would have calculated the EMA as .053 for the week of 10/26/07.

B: This calculation involves handling negative numbers as well as positive numbers. Because there were only 1,179 advances and 2,350 declines, the difference between them is a negative number—specifically, –1171. Therefore, the weekly breadth reading for the week of 11/2/07 is calculated as follows:

–1171/3588 = –.3264 or –32.64%

C: The formula to create the new six-week exponential moving average for the week ending November 2, 2007, uses the data from Table 5.1 to make the following calculations:

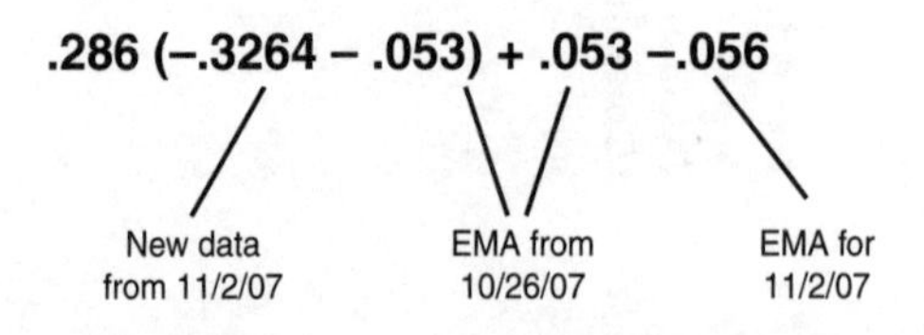

D: 670 – 2870 = –2200 (Adv-Dec differential). –2200/3577 = –.6150 or –61.50%.

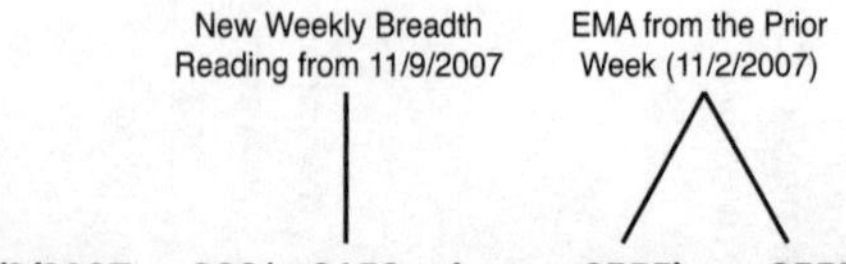

E: **New .286 EMA for 11/9/2007 = .286(–.6150 minus –.0555) + –.0555.**

New .286 EMA = .286(–.0.56) + –.055.

New .286 EMA = –.1602 + -.055 = –.2152 or –21.5%.

Summing Up

You have now learned how to locate and to organize the data required to maintain the Weekly Breadth Reading and the six-week exponential moving average of the Weekly Breadth Reading—an explanation that takes far longer to read and to understand than it will take you to actually carry out the process each week, once you have become more conversant with the procedures involved.

We will be moving along in a moment to the interpretation of the data you have learned how to maintain, and to the exciting performance record of this indicator.

Should you want further information regarding exponential averages and their construction, you can visit my firm's website at www.systemsandforecasts.com or do a search of the Internet for the following topic: "exponential averages, calculation of." There are numerous websites that discuss exponential averages from various points of view.

Buy and Sell Signals Generated by the Six-Week EMA of the Weekly Breadth Reading

Although the calculations involved in maintaining the data required for the six-week EMA of the Weekly Breadth Reading appear complicated until their routine becomes familiar, the signal triggers—there are only two—are actually quite straightforward.

Buy (or hold, if you are already invested) signals are generated when the six-week EMA of the Weekly Breadth Reading rises to above .25 or 25%.

After a buy signal has been generated, you hold your positions until the six-week EMA of the Weekly Breadth Reading declines to –.05 (–5%) or below; at which time, you become free to sell if Bond-Stock Valuation Models are no longer in their most favorable position.

There is an exception, however: If both Bond-Stock Valuation Models decline into their most bearish zones, sell at that point regardless of the position of the six-week EMA of the Weekly Breadth Reading traded.

Final Review

The Concept of the Weekly Breadth Signal

The Weekly Breadth Signal is based upon the concept that when market breadth becomes extremely favorable, the ratio of advancing to declining issues is extremely high, the odds are that the bulls have seriously taken charge and that the stock market is likely to advance and to continue to advance until market breadth is no longer favorable.

Based on our historical studies dating back to the early 1970s, such favorable indications take place when the six-week exponential of the Weekly Breadth Readings ("Breadth Signal") reaches or rises above .25 or 25%.

For example, if on a one-week basis, there were 2,500 advances, 1,500 declines, and 3,700 issues traded, the weekly ratio would be 1,000 net advances (2500 up – 1500 down), divided by 3,700 issues traded—a ratio of .27 or 27%.

Remember, although this would be a strongly positive ratio, a six-week exponential average that reaches that high would be required to generate a Weekly Breadth Buy Signal, not simply a one-week reading.

Buy signals do not occur all that often; the stock market does not produce this sort of positive consistency all that frequently. When they do occur, they tend to produce very favorable results.

Exception to Buy-and-Hold Rule

Buy-and/or-hold signals derived from Weekly Breadth Signals should NOT be respected when both the Baa-based Bond-Stock Valuation *and* the Treasury Bond-Stock Valuation Models are in their most bearish zones; such periods have historically proved on balance to be too bearish, even in the face of positive Weekly Breadth Signals.

At all other times, even if just one of the Bond-Stock Valuation Models is no worse than neutral, all Weekly Breadth Buy Signals should be followed. After a Weekly Breadth Buy Signal has taken place, stock market positions should be held until cancellation signals develop.

Cancellation Signals

Cancellation signals do not necessarily indicate that stock market positions should be totally liquidated. They do indicate that the major bullish indication for stocks that has been generated by the most recent Weekly Breadth Signal is no longer operative and that sell signals, if any are operative (based on Bond-Stock Valuation Models), should be followed.

Cancellation signals are considered to have taken place and favorable signals from breadth readings are no longer operative, when the six-week EMA of the Weekly Breadth Readings falls from above –.05 (for example, –0.3 or +.04) to –.05 or below (for example, –.07 or –.15).

Readings in the order of "0" or –.05 to –.10, or even somewhat lower, are not necessarily bearish. Such readings, indicating that the percentages of rising and falling stocks are more or less balanced, reflect a more neutral stock market.

Cancellation signals are basically cancellations of strong buy-hold indications, rather than necessarily signals of imminent market decline and are not, in and of themselves, indications to heavily liquidate stocks.

The management of portfolios is discussed in subsequent chapters.

The Historical Performance Record of Breadth Signals

(Note: The performance tables that appear in this section do not include the influence of Bond-Stock Valuation considerations. They are based purely upon advance-decline relationships to the number of issues traded on the New York Stock Exchange.)

The past performance record of the Breadth Signals has been quite impressive. Let's start with a summary of the performance results going as far back as 1970—nearly 38 years of historical data—and then examine the trade-by-trade performance for this period.

Trade dates are presumed to be the first days of the subsequent week, rather than the last days of the previous week, even though signals are based on last-day data.

Although buy-sell signals are based upon weekly data, generally through Friday, we are using the following first days of the subsequent week (usually Monday), as our hypothetical trade dates. Realistically, investors would not have the week-ending data required to construct signals until after the close on Friday, which is too late to transact. There is a slight amount of performance degeneration as a result of delaying hypothetical performance by one trading day, but resulting performance data does become more honest and representative of what a trader might actually encounter in the real-life application of this indicator.

Table 5.2 provides a quick summary of results from January 1970 to November 16, 2007.

TABLE 5.2
Breadth Signals

	% of Time Invested	Years Invested	Buy and Hold	Gain per Annum Weekly Impulse	Gain per Annum While Invested	Open Drawdown
37.9 Years—January 1970–December 2007						
NYSE Index	24.8% A	9.4	8.0% B	4.7% C	20.1% D	11.1% E
S & P 500	24.8%	9.4	7.6%	4.1%	17.5%	14.6%
26.7 Years—January 1981–December 2007						
NYSE Index	26.5%	7.1	9.6%	4.9%	19.7%	–11.1%
S & P 500	26.5%	7.1	9.2%	4.2%	16.9%	–14.6%

Notes from Table 5.2

A: The Breadth Signal would have kept investors in the stock market for a total of 9.4 years, or 24.8% of the 37.9 year period.

B: Investors who had remained fully invested in the NYSE Index over the 37.9-year period would have achieved a rate of return of 8.0% per annum.

C: Investors who had been invested in the NYSE Index only during the 9.4 years that Breadth Signals had been in effect would have achieved a rate of return of 4.7% over the 37.9 years. This would have come to 58.8% of the total gain achieved by buy-and-hold investment strategies, while being at risk only 24.8% of the time.

D: Capital appreciated at a rate of 20.1% a year while invested, or at a rate of 251% of the rate of return of buy-and-hold strategies. Of the 8.0% annualized rate of return of buy-and-hold strategies, 4.7% was achieved during the 24.8% of the time that Breadth Signals were in effect. The remaining 3.3% of return each year was achieved during the 75.2% of the time that Breadth Signals were not in effect. The stock market advanced at a rate of 4.4% per annum during periods that Weekly Breadth Signals were not in effect, basically at the rate of money market funds, give or take. On balance, there has been relatively little benefit in being in the stock market when Breadth Signals have not been in effect.

E: The worst drawdowns or maximum losses while being invested during periods that Breadth Signals have been in effect would have been 11.1% for the New York Stock Exchange Index or 14.6% for the Standard & Poor's 500 Index. These represent very low-risk levels, particularly when compared to buy-and-hold strategies with these indices, which have involved possible drawdowns in the order of 47–48%.

You may wonder why I have shown two starting dates for the Weekly Breadth Readings, 1970 and 1981. The historical data upon which this indicator was developed was available for our research purposes as far back as 1970, which is the starting period we employed in the back testing of this indicator. However, Bond-Stock Valuation Models that we employ in conjunction with Weekly Impulse Signals have been effective only since 1981; thus, you have also been provided with the performance of the Weekly Impulse Signal component of the combined Bond-Stock Valuation Model and Weekly Impulse Signals for the same overlapping 26.7 years, 1981–2007.

Figure 5.3 and Table 5.3 illustrate the relationship of the Weekly Impulse levels and the price movement of the New York Stock Exchange Index.

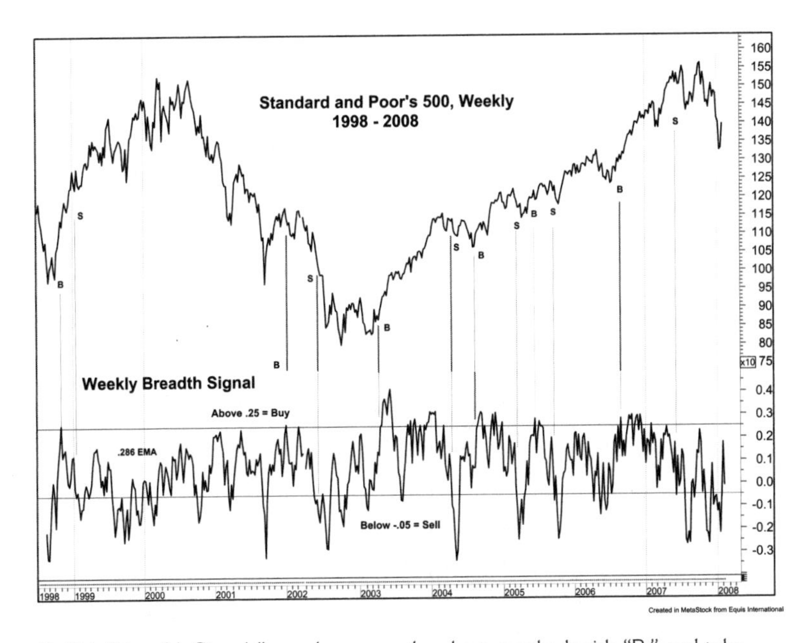

Bullish "Breadth Signals" are shown on the chart, marked with "B," and take place when the Breadth Signals rise to above 25%. Sell signals take place when the Breadth Signals decline to –5% or below. Not all signals are shown. Most signals have been profitable, but an entry toward the end of 2001 proved to be unproductive.

Figure 5.3

New York Stock Exchange Index and six-week EMA of the Weekly Breadth Readings.

TABLE 5.3

Trade-by-Trade Performance of the Breadth Signal
New York Stock Exchange Index (1970–2007)
Trading First Day of Week on Signals Generated the Last Day of Previous Week

Buy Date	Buy Price	Sell Date	Sell Price	Gain/ Loss	$100 Becomes	% Gain	%Loss
700908	478.67	701026	480.05	0.29%	100.29	0.29%	
701207	517.48	710510	596.15	15.20%	115.53	15.20	
720110	604.50	720327	631.57	4.48%	120.71	4.48	
731001	617.72	731105	599.64	–2.93%	117.18		–2.93
750113	406.45	750407	451.39	11.06%	130.13	11.06	
760112	539.15	760412	563.90	4.59%	136.10	4.59	
761213	595.83	770228	573.41	–3.76%	130.98		–3.76
780807	615.39	780925	606.72	–1.41%	129.14		–1.41
790820	655.78	791001	653.99	–0.29%	128.76		–0.29
800519	649.12	801027	780.55	20.25%	154.84	20.25	
820830	713.94	830711	1030.30	44.31%	223.45	44.31	
850121	1069.22	850812	1149.05	7.47%	240.13	7.47	
851118	1211.01	860623	1487.62	22.84%	294.98	22.84	
870209	1679.43	870413	1714.42	2.08%	301.12	2.08	
880307	1591.66	880418	1551.91	–2.50%	293.60		–2.50

Buy Date	Buy Price	Sell Date	Sell Price	Gain/ Loss	$100 Becomes	% Gain	%Loss
910204	2011.97	910624	2151.75	6.95%	314.00	6.95	
920106	2430.37	920330	2357.84	−2.98%	304.63		−2.98
930208	2612.45	931108	2693.34	3.10%	314.06	3.10	
970609	4759.98	971103	5208.94	9.43%	343.68	9.43	
981109	5912.20	990125	6196.84	4.81%	360.23	4.81	
20020107	6271.81	020610	5851.40	−6.70%	336.08		−6.70
20030428	5108.24	030804	5515.68	7.98%	362.89	7.98	
20030908	5805.60	040419	6620.05	14.03%	413.80	14.03	
20040830	6414.54	050321	7229.20	12.70%	466.35	12.70	
20050620	7325.69	050926	7556.45	3.15%	481.04	3.15	
20060905	8452.96	070611	9841.73	16.43%	560.07	16.43	
				Avg. Gain/loss +7.33%		Avg. Gain +11.11%	Avg. Loss −2.94%

Notes from Table 5.3

There were 19 (73.1%) winning trades, and 7 (26.9%) losing trades. The average winning trade was 3.78 times the percentage size of the average losing trade.

10.25 to 1 gain:loss ratio! The odds have been better than 10:1 in favor of the investor.

There were 19 winning trades, averaging 11.11% per trade, for a total percentage gain of 211.09%. There were seven losing trades, averaging 2.94% per trade, for a total percentage loss of 20.58%.

The total percentage gain (211.09%) exceeded the total percentage loss (20.58%) by a ratio of 10.25. For every one percent loss as a result of using this model, 10.25% was gained!

The Breadth Signal clearly did not capture every advance made by the stock market between 1970–2007. However, once again, it did capture nearly 59% of the total gain achieved during that period while being invested less than 25% of the time.

Investments in the stock market made on the basis of breadth buy signals, and held only until cancellation signals were generated, produced gain:loss ratios, again, of better than 10:1.

There would have been very little lost, on balance, by investors who maintained assets in the stock market only while buy-hold signals were in effect and who moved into money market instruments at other times.

Final Thoughts

The Breadth Signal, and its attendant action levels, are well worth the following. I and my staff have employed it for years in support of other indicators that we employ and as its own signal device.

(Ongoing levels of Breadth Signals, as well as the Bond-Stock Valuation Models, may be found in the newsletter, Systems and Forecasts, which also provides rosters of strongly performing mutual and exchange traded funds. Free trials may be secured at www.systemsandforecasts.com.)

Let's move along now to see how combining this indicator with our Bond-Stock Valuation Models produces a synergy that outperforms any single one of the models in our repertoire, when taken on its own.

CHAPTER 6

INDICATOR SYNERGY PLUS

Improving Rates of Return Still Further by Coordinating Weekly Breadth Thrust Readings with Bond-Stock Valuation Models

Chapter 4, "Achieving a 92.59% Profit Ratio," demonstrated how the performance of even an excellent, single indicator can be improved by combining that indicator with another. The result was the Twin Bond-Stock Valuation Model, which gained even when invested only 50% of the time—more than buy-and-hold strategies, which carry risk 100% of the time.

This chapter shows how to improve on the Twin Bond-Stock Valuation Model by combining its signals with the Weekly Breadth Signal. This new creation is the Twin Breadth Bond-Stock Valuation Model (TWIBBS). The Twin Bond-Stock Valuation Model compares monetary conditions with corporate earnings. These have correlations with the performance of the stock market, which is influenced by interest rates.

Characteristics of TWIBBS

The stock market anticipates news and changes direction *before* significant developments take place. It is dangerous to take action based on comments on financial news programs made in response to current news, rather than in advance of news to come.

Because the stock market tends to act on anticipated news, stocks may turn up strongly in advance of favorable news, such as declines in interest rates. So, the Twin Bond-Stock Valuation Model may produce its buy signals *following* indications of market strength. Weekly Breadth Signals, based upon studies of how many stocks are actually rising in price compared to the number declining in price, sometimes give more timely market entries. Entries generated by Weekly Breadth Signals tend to be reliable and to accurately produce more gain even in the absence of the most favorable readings of the Twin Bond-Stock Valuation Model, which sometimes occur following rather than preceding Weekly Breadth Signals.

Hold signals generated by the Weekly Breadth Signal are reliable, even if both Bond-Stock Valuation Models have fallen from their most bullish condition to neutral. The numbers of trades tend to be reduced, profitable trades extended, and minor whipsaws minimized if positions are held until the Weekly Breadth Signal produces a sell signal.

The following procedures create a composite timing model to produce superior results.

The Procedures for Maintaining and Interpreting TWIBBS

At the end of each week, compute the readings of the Baa Bond-Stock Valuation Model, the U.S. Government Bond-Stock Valuation Model, and the weekly Exponential Moving Average (EMA) from the previous chapter:

1. If TWIBBS has been out of the market, enter on the first of the following signals: a) either Bond-Stock Valuation Model improves sufficiently to enter its most bullish zone; or b) the EMA of the weekly net ratio stands above .25 or

25%. This buy signal should be followed unless both Bond-Stock Valuation Models are in their most bearish zones.

2. Consider a stock market buy and/or hold status to be in effect until the following takes place:
   - The EMA of the Weekly Ratio falls to –.05 (–5%) or below.

     and
   - Both weekly Bond-Stock Valuation Models have fallen from below their most bullish zones.

     or
   - Both weekly Bond-Stock Valuation Models have declined to their most bearish zones.
3. If a TWIBBS hold is closed out because both weekly Bond-Stock valuation models have declined to their most bearish zones, consider a market re-entry signal to have taken place if either weekly model returns to its most bullish zone, regardless of the status of the Weekly Breadth Signal.

The EMA of the Weekly Breadth level must once again reach .25 (25%) to generate a re-entry signal, presuming that both Bond-Stock Valuation Models remain above their most bearish zones.

One bullish signal puts you into stocks, but all three bullish signals must be cancelled to generate a sell.

Evaluating the Benefits of TWIBBS

Compare the results of trading via TWIBBS to trading via the Twin Bond-Stock Valuation Model alone (see Tables 6.1 and 6.2).

TABLE 6.1 *TWIBBS*

Percent of Time Invested	# of Entries	# of Winning Entries	Average % Gain	# of Losing Entries	Average % Loss	Avg., All Entries	Annualized Return	Return While Invested	Maximum Drawdown
58.2%	33	27 (81.8%)	13.4%	6 (18.2%)	–1.8%	+10.64%	11.6%	20.7%	–16.7%

TABLE 6.2 *Twin Bond-Stock Valuation Model*

Percent of Time Invested	# of Entries	# of Winning Entries	Average % Gain	# of Losing Entries	Average % Loss	Avg., All Entries	Annualized Return	Return While Invested	Maximum Drawdown
50.5%	39	28 (71.8%)	11.2%	11 (28.2%)	–1.2%	+7.7%	+ 9.7%	20.0%	–16.7%

The Final Tally—TWIBBS Wins Hands Down

By almost every measure, investors benefit from the TWIBBS Timing Model. Check the roster of comparative data:

- Although invested for a larger percentage of the time (58.2%) versus (50.5%), TWIBBS had only 33 entries. The Twin Bond-Stock Valuation Model had 39 entries. The fewer the entries required for the same gross profit, the better.
- TWIBBS achieved a higher ratio of profitable trades than the Twin Bond-Stock Valuation Timing Model: 81.8% versus 71.8%. The average result per trade for TWIBBS was a gain of 10.65%. The average result per trade for the Twin Bond-Stock Valuation Timing Model was a gain of 7.7%.
- TWIBBS achieved a higher average percentage gain per winning trade: 13.4% versus 11.2%.
- TWIBBS showed a lower percentage of losses: 18.8% versus 28.2%.
- TWIBBS showed a higher annualized rate of return: +11.6% versus +9.7%.
- The maximum drawdown for TWIBBS was the same as the Twin Bond-Stock Valuation Model, 16.7%. The additional profit in TWIBBS did not cause greater risk.

Although TWIBBS produced a lower percentage of losses than the Twin Bond-Stock Valuation Timing Model, the average size of the losses was slightly larger: 1.8% for TWIBBS, and only 1.2% for the Twin Bond-Stock Valuation Model.

The rate of return for TWIBBS was 20.7% per year, slightly higher than the annualized rate of return of the Twin Bond-Stock Valuation Model. The outperformance by TWIBBS resulted from being invested for greater productive periods of time.

Final Thoughts

The varying models are not opposites. TWIBBS is the Twin Bond-Stock Valuation Model plus the application of the Weekly Breadth Signal. This model frequently places you into the market sooner than the Twin Bond-Stock Valuation Model, and sometimes keeps you in longer with fewer interruptions.

A Stock Market Power Gauge

The combination of the status of indicators that comprise TWIBBS may be thought of as a Stock Market Power Gauge. If none of the indicators lies in favorable position, then the gauge is producing low readings[md]stay out of the stock market. If only one of the Bond-Stock Valuation Models is favorable, then the gauge has inched up somewhat. If both Bond-Stock Valuation Models are favorable, or if a Weekly Breadth Signal has been triggered, then the needle on the gauge has moved into positive territory. If Weekly Breadth Signals are in effect and if both Bond-Stock Valuation Models are in favorable areas, then the Stock Market Power Gauge stands at its maximum, most positive, levels. The risks are low and profit potentials are high.

This completes the array of market timing indicators required to outperform the market, the majority of mutual funds, and most other investors. Later chapters discuss portfolio maintenance, the selection of investments, and ways to combine information to create portfolios that evolve with personal and financial changes over your lifetime.

CHAPTER 7

CREATING THE BEST BLENDS OF RISK AND REWARD IN YOUR PORTFOLIO

You want to be invested in stocks during the strongest periods and the least invested during the weakest periods.

Even so, money tends to flow into the market following strong advances, rather than as market advances are just getting under way. Fortunately, your new timing models have excellent performance records to help you beat the crowd.

This chapter discusses how to allocate your assets between stocks and more conservative investments—an ongoing and ever-varying decision.

The balance between stocks, bonds, and other investments should be dynamic—changing as your age and life situations change. Different allocations work best for different life periods and market climates. **You can position yourself to secure considerable reductions in risk while maximizing your profit opportunities.**

Table 7.1 summarizes the performance data of the six timing models previously covered.

TABLE 7.1 *Compilation of Performance—New York Stock Exchange Index*

Various Indicator Models (1981–2007)

Indicator Model	% of Time Invested	% of Entries Profitable	% Un-profitable	Avg. Gain	Avg. Loss	Avg. Result	Annualized Rate of Return	Return While Invested	Maximum Drawdown
Baa Bond-Stock Val. (A)	37.0%	86.7%	13.3%	8.1 %	–2.1%	+7.3%	+7.1%	20.4%	–11.1%
Treasury Bond-Stock Val. (A)	38.6%	72.2%	27.8%	9.1%	–1.2%	+6.3%	+ 7.4%	20.1%	–16.7%
Baa + Treasury Bullish (B)	24.9%	92.6%	7.4%	6.0%	–2.8%	+5.4%	+4.5%	20.8%	–11.1%
Baa or Treasury Bullish (C)	50.7%	71.8%	28.2%	11.2%	–1.2%	+7.7%	+9.7%	20.0%	–16.7%
Weekly Breadth Signal (D)	26.9%	81.3%	18.8%	11.9%	–4.1%	+8.9%	+4.9%	19.7%	–11.1%
TWIBBS	58.2%	81.8%	18.2%	13.4%	–1.8%	+10.7%	+11.6%	20.7%	–16.7%

Notes

(A) Based on time spent in most bullish zones only.

(B) Both Baa and Treasury Bond-Stock Valuation Models must be in most favorable zones.

(C) Either Baa or Treasury Bond-Stock Valuation Models may be in most favorable zones.

(D) From the time the most favorable Weekly Breadth Signal enters buy-hold position to the cancellation of hold signal. When applied within TWIBBS, certain conditions apply that improve the performance of the Weekly Breadth Signal indicator.

"Annualized Rate of Return" is profit on a full-year basis for this particular signal. For example, the Baa Bond-Stock Valuation Model, which is invested 36.6% of the time, produced average annual returns of +7.2%.

"Return While Invested" is the rate at which gains are achieved. For example, the Baa Bond-Stock Valuation Model produced profit of 548.73% while in the market 9.8 of the 26.8 years between 1981–2007. The rate of return was 21.0%, per annum or twice the rate of return of buy-and-hold.

"Maximum Drawdown" is the worst interim loss taken by following this model, before profits reached new all-time highs. This is a measure of the minimum past risk of trading by this model.

All the timing models have excellent risk/reward ratios over a quarter of a century. Next, examine additional measurements of past performance.

Risk-Return Relationships of Buy-and-Hold Portfolios over the Years

Table 7.2 shows risk-return relationships for investment portfolios including stocks and bonds, both maintained on a buy-and-hold basis, from 1956–2005 (source: Ibbotson Presentation Materials © 2006).

TABLE 7.2 *Rates of Return and Risk Levels, Stock-Bond Portfolio Allocations*

Stock—Standard & Poor's 500 Index; Bonds—U.S. Intermediate Government

Percent Stocks	Percent Bonds	Annual Returns Highest	Average	Lowest
100	0	+41.1%	+10.3%	–24.9%
90	10	+38.9	+10.2	–23.3
80	20	+34.4	+9.9	–20.0
70	30	+31.2	+9.6	–16.8
60	40	+29.2	+9.3	–13.6
50	50	+27.1	+8.9	–10.4
40	60	+26.0	+8.6	–7.2
30	70	+26.8	+8.1	–4.0
20	80	+27.6	+7.7	–3.9
10	90	+28.3	+7.2	–4.5
0	100	+29.1	+6.8	–5.1

The table is an historical evaluation of buy-and-hold investment portfolios with ratios of assets of stocks, represented by the Standard & Poor's 500 Index and bonds, represented by the relatively low-risk, 10-year intermediate U.S. Government treasury bond. The highest single year returns of portfolios of the ratios of bonds and stocks is shown, and the average performance of different blends and the largest historical risk levels are shown.

In the analysis of timing indicators (refer to Table 7.1), "Maximum Drawdowns" represent more stringent tests of risk than "Lowest Annual Returns," because losses during bear markets often spread over more than just one year. They exceed losses taken in any single year. Also, because the worst drawdowns are the moments of greatest loss, they are unlikely to take place right at year's end. To this extent, Table 7.2 underestimates actual historical risk levels.

Analysis of Table 7.2: The Best Pockets of Investment Blends

It might be difficult to tolerate the risk of a portfolio 100% committed to stocks. Between 1956–2005, portfolios fully invested in the Standard & Poor's 500 Index had their best year at +41.1%, an average annual gain of +10.3%, but a greatest single-year loss of 24.9%.

Why Not Losing Is More Important Than Winning

Portfolios fully committed to stocks would be the best performing of the portfolio mixes. However, actual losses of 24.9% can be ruinous to a retired investor, living off his assets. For example, suppose that you begin the given year with $100,000 of assets, and at the start of each year, you withdrew $7,000 for living expenses. If your portfolio lost 24.9%, your assets shrink from $100,000 to $75,100. Then another $7,000 would be deducted for the year following, leaving you with just $68,100 to start the coming year.

To continue to maintain the $7,000 cash flow for living expenses (not even adjusted for inflation), you would have to earn an annual return of at least 10.3% per year from your remaining $68,100 just to maintain the level of your portfolio. One more bad year, and the task might prove to be impossible. (Incidentally, with only $68,100, you would have to gain 46.8% to return to your starting level of $100,000.)

It is more important to avoid losses than to secure profit. If you lose 50%, you need to make 100% to return to the breakeven point. It does not matter whether the loss or the profit comes first. For example, if you start with $100,000 and lose $50,000 (50%), you need to make 100% profit from the remaining $50,000 to return to $100,000. If you start with $100,000, and make 100% to double to $200,000, a loss of just 50% brings you back to the original level. This math does not even consider any draws for living expenses, so the actual breakeven requirements are more severe.

If you lose 25%, you need to make 33 ⅓% to break even—presuming that you do not have to draw from your assets for living expenses. If you lose 15%, you need to make 17.65% to break even. And, if you lose 77%—as the NASDAQ Composite Index did between 2000–2002—you need to make more than 334% to break even—something the NASDAQ Composite did not even approach between 2002 through 2007.

Back to the Table

You may be able to afford the risk of being fully invested in stocks. For example, if you are employed with discretionary income AND if one or the other of the strongest of timing models are favorably situated, you might choose to remain fully invested in stocks.

The typical buy-and-hold investor, however, is probably better off maintaining between 30%–80% of assets in stocks, rather than 100%. Review Table 7.2. At a portfolio ratio of 60% stocks to 40% bonds, the average annual return to investors was 9.3%; this is only 1% per year less than portfolios invested 100% in stocks, which returned, on average, 10.3% per year. However, the maximum risk level involved with a 60% to 40% portfolio was only 13.6% compared to 24.9%—just a little over one-half the annual risk of being invested 100% in stocks.

Conservative investors, those who cannot emotionally accept or afford large losses, will find that portfolios with as little as 30% in stocks may meet their needs with historical rates of return of 8.1% per year, and historical maximum annual losses of 4.0%. In effect, compared to being fully invested in stocks, with a 30% stock to 70% bond mix, you would have given up 21.4% of your average profit (10.3% per year down to 8.1% per year), but secured an 83.9% reduction in your risk (24.9% down to 4.0%).

Here are the conclusions from these numbers: The best mutual funds for many investors are funds whose portfolios are conservatively structured, usually in the order of 60% stocks to 40% bonds. Conservative mutual funds, which hold equity as low as 20% to 30%, have often been steady and satisfactory performers with relatively low downside risk. The greater risks of volatile mutual funds and stocks are not necessarily justified by greater returns.

How the Timing Models Allow You to Take Greater Risks, While Maintaining a High Degree of Safety

Table 7.3 summarizes the annual performance of TWIBBS between 1994–2006, compared to the buy-and-hold performance of the New York Stock Exchange Index.

TABLE 7.3 *The New York Stock Exchange Index*

TWIBBS versus Buy and Hold 1994–2007

Year	TWIBBS NYSE Index	$100,000 Becomes	Buy and Hold NYSE Index	$100,000 Becomes
1994	–0.47%	$99,530	–3.14%	$96,860
1995	+31.31%	130,693	+31.31%	127,187
1996	+19.06%	155,603	+19.06%	151,429
1997	+22.23%	190,194	+30.31%	197,327
1998	+30.59%	248,374	+16.55%	229,984
1999	–1.64%	244,301	+ 9.15%	251,028
2000	No trades	244,301	+1.01%	253,563
2001	+12.36%	274,496	–10.21%	227,674
2002	+1.66%	279,052	–19.83%	182,527
2003	+29.28%	360,759	+29.28%	235,970
2004	+12.16%	404,627	+12.16%	264,664
2005	+6.95%	432,749	+6.95%	283,058
2006	+17.86%	510,038	+17.86%	333,612
2007	+6.58%	543,598	+6.58%	355,563
Averages	**+13.42%**	**$543,598**	**+10.50%**	**$355,564**

The Magic of Consistency, Compounding, and Loss Avoidance

During this period, the ratio of average annual return, 13.42% for TWIBBS divided by 10.50% for buy-and-hold strategies, was

1.28. The average annual advantage for TWIBBS over buy-and-hold was 28.0%.

However, the ratio of account values at the end of the period was 1.529 in favor of TWIBBS ($543,598 divided by $355,564), illustrating the benefits of steady compounding at higher rates of return coupled with loss avoidance.

Although no charges were made against TWIBBS for trading expenses, no credit was given to the TWIBBS account for interest received during the approximately 40% of the time that TWIBBS was not in the stock market.

The period listed in Table 7.3 was above average for TWIBBS performance compared to buy-and-hold strategies, largely because of the severity of the 2000–2002 bear market. However, TWIBBS has outperformed buy-and-hold strategies for more than a quarter century.

Which Portfolio Mix Fits You?

Although some investors prefer to be fully invested at times, few investors or mutual funds hold 100% of assets in stocks at any given time. If you refer back to Table 7.2, while a reduction of the ratio of stocks to the entire portfolio from 100% to 80% lowers your average annual gain by less than 4% (10.3% to 9.9%), it reduces your one-year historical risk from 24.9% to 20%, a favorable change of 19.7% in risk level.

TWIBBS had maximum drawdowns of 16.7% (through 2007), much lower than maximum buy-and-hold drawdowns of the Standard & Poor's 500 Index, which has been above 47% during full-scale bear markets. If TWIBBS investors maintained a 20% income position, the risks of investing via TWIBBS declined from 16.7% to 13.0%, still too high for some people, but actually low in terms of risks associated with stocks.

Are You Young, Rich, Aggressive, and Handsome? (Just Kidding About the Last One)

Financial planners like to speak of the "accumulation phase of life" and the "distribution phase of life."

The accumulation phase is when you are able to grow your assets—as your income rises, and as your investments grow, you may have a surplus of income over expenses to place into your portfolio.

During the early portion of your accumulation period, you start with a small but rapidly growing asset base, with many years for your assets to accumulate. **This is a period when you are most likely to take chances and to invest aggressively.**

You are also able to afford to invest large percentages of your assets in stocks. Your positions are likely to emphasize growth rather than the preservation of capital. Because your initial asset base is not large, losses will not threaten your future.

Growing the Family—Accumulation Slows

Accumulation slows or even stops during the years of child rearing, home buying, college costs, payments for weddings, and child subsidies involved in birthing, raising, and assisting children.

Risk control increases during this period, unless you are one of the fortunate minority whose assets and income exceed the expenses of life.

Most families, in this stage, should reduce stock investments to the 60% level, and establish portfolios with holdings to provide predictable returns, such as TIPS (treasury inflation-protected securities, 10-year notes, guaranteed by the U.S. government, whose annual face value and interest payout increase each year at the rate of inflation). Check the Internet for further information regarding TIPS, the only investment guaranteed by the U.S. government to outperform inflation. This is particularly suited for tax-deferred accounts. Diversified portfolios of high-quality tax-exempt bonds are another popular choice for this purpose, if your income places you in the highest tax brackets.

The Nest Is Empty—A Final Burst of Accumulation

For many couples, the years preceding full retirement are a strong period for the accumulation of capital. The years between ages 45–65 are the period of their highest earnings, and are also a time when expenses for children decline. Many spouses return to employment, hoping to resume old careers or to start new careers, which brings in additional income.

Planning for Retirement Needs

In considering your likely capital needs for a comfortable retirement, evaluate the following:

- If a couple is 65 years of age, the odds are approximately even that at least one of the couple will live to be more than 90 years of age. Retirement assets may have to last longer than you think.
- Do not forget to allow for the effects of loss of buying power due to inflation. If annual inflation averages just 3% per year, at the end of 15 years, the buying power of $1,000 today will be reduced to just $633.

Estimate returns from your investments conservatively. Investment returns from stock and real estate investment have both averaged approximately 10% per year, although they do not take place at the same time. For example, the two decades between 1980 and 1999 were the two best back-to-back decades for the stock market since the start of the twentieth century. However, values of real estate declined precipitously during 2007–2008. Rates of return from the stock market were barely positive during the period between 2000–2008.

You do not want your expenses to exceed income in any given year, and certainly not over a series of years. But you can outperform buy-and-hold investment strategies if you apply the investment techniques shown in previous chapters.

The ultimate goal in preparing for retirement is to accumulate assets 20 to 40 times your annual living expenses. This allows for maintenance of your capital, inflationary factors, and taxation on your profits, while allowing for withdrawal of 5% per year for living expenses. If you are short of these goals at the time of retirement, you might have to postpone the time of retirement until you approach the minimum goal.

A Typical Recommendation to Our Clients

Place a high priority in your planning on maximizing your assets, but not on maximizing risk. If you have already accumulated more assets than you need to comfortably meet your projected expenses, you may want to increase risk levels of a portion of your assets, but not of the base required for safety. Investments should be well-diversified geographically (your portfolio should include international stocks and/or bonds), as well as by risk level.

Retirement Period

This is the distribution period—the time when you will not add assets, but will begin to draw to meet expenses.

Your goal is to make those assets productive enough to provide the income stream you need without reducing your base of capital. **Because you can no longer work to replace losses, the highest of priorities is the avoidance of unacceptable risks.** Your portfolio should be weighted toward high-quality, low-risk income investments. Portfolio blends that replicate a 30% stock–70% bond allocation are generally the blends of choice during this period of life.

How TWIBBS and Other Timing Models Can Be Employed to Help You Increase Your Rates of Return Without Increasing Risk Levels

Readers are referred to Table 7.1 to reference data involved in the following discussions.

A Quick Review of the Features of All the Timing Models

Let's review some salient features of the timing models, presuming that the performance of your stock portfolios will be equal to the performance of broadly based market indices, such as the New York Stock Exchange Index and the Standard & Poor's 500 Index:

- **All the timing models produce higher rates of return while you are invested than buy-and-hold strategies.** Rates of return while invested range from 19.7% to 20.8% per year. The average annual rate of return on a buy-and-hold basis for the New York Stock Exchange Index during the 1981–2007 period was 9.61%.

- **All the timing models have lower levels of risk than buy-and-hold strategies.** TWIBBS produced the highest rates of annual returns of all our models. It involves risk considerably below the maximum risks of constant investment in stocks.
- **All the timing models have excellent ratios of profitable to unprofitable market entries, ranging from a low of 71.8% to a high of 86.7%.** The odds are extremely favorable for investors.

The Bottom Line—Added Safety May Also Mean Added Opportunity

During 2002, the New York Stock Exchange Index incurred a loss of 19.83%—tolerable, perhaps, for an investor during the "accumulation period," but very difficult for investors in the "distribution" or retirement period.

More Aggressive Investing via TWIBBS

Suppose you had been operating on the basis of TWIBBS during 2002. TWIBBS managed to produce a slight gain, +1.66%, during that bearish year—its rules keeping you out of the stock market during the majority of time that stocks were declining.

Lowest-Risk Investing

Suppose that your assets provide sufficient income from conservative investments. You would like to secure something extra, but you are risk averse. Table 7.1 shows that when the

Baa + U.S. Government Bond-Stock Valuation Models are BOTH in their most favorable zones, the odds were 12.5:1 (92.6% versus 7.4%) that stocks would rise.

If you had waited for these conditions as a prerequisite for investing in stocks, you would have been at risk less than 25% of the time, and would have achieved profits at a rate of nearly 21% per year during the periods when you are invested. You would have secured just about one-half the return from being in the stock market all the time, while being at risk less than 25% of the time. Your maximum drawdown would have been only 11.1%, which falls by 3%-4% per year by the income you receive during the nine months you are out of stocks. (It goes without saying that future performance may not equal the past, but then again, it might surpass the past.)

A Risk Compromise

If you prefer a model with fine historical rates of return and excellent past risk levels, make your greatest investments in stocks when either the Baa Bond-Stock Valuation Model OR the U.S. Government Bond-Stock Valuation Model lie in their most favorable zones. Risks were low at –16.7% maximum drawdown between 1981–2007.

Mixing Timing Models with Buy and Hold for Timely Increases in Portfolio Positions

Because many investors prefer to hold some stock positions for favorable tax treatment, it is possible to maintain a 30% allocation in stocks, mutual funds, or exchange-traded funds (ETFs) on a long-term basis—Table 7.2 shows past risk levels—while maintaining additional positions only during periods that the safest of the timing models flash the green light.

Seek an approach favoring the maintenance of a core of invested positions in mutual funds with good long-term performance, adding more aggressive holdings during periods of favorable risk-reward relationships. This is a good strategy for almost all investors and in just about all market climates. With this strategy, you establish fluid levels of stock holdings whose exposures increase and decrease in accordance with time-proven market indicators.

Because risk levels decrease during periods of favorable signals, you may increase your allocation of stock positions at such times. For example, if you conservatively maintain 30% stock positions on a buy-and-hold basis, you should be able to increase these holdings to 50%–60% stocks when Bond-Stock Valuation Models and TWIBBS are most favorable. If you maintain 50%–60% stocks on a buy-and-hold basis, these proportions may be raised to 70%–80% during favorable periods.

The next chapter introduces additional strategies that enable you to outperform random buy-and-hold tactics in the selection of your investments.

CHAPTER 8

PUTTING TOGETHER YOUR WINNING INVESTMENT PORTFOLIO

The First Step: Diversification

Increasing return while reducing risk has been the emphasis of previous chapters. The strategies have demonstrated that you can profit by timing your entries and exits so that your largest positions are taken when the odds are favorable, and the smallest positions assumed when the odds are least favorable. By establishing portfolio blends between equities and income, you can control risks.

In the final section of the book, which begins with this chapter, emphasis shifts to show how specifically selecting stocks, bonds, mutual funds, and exchange-traded funds (ETFs) may be employed to create blended portfolios to ensure maximum profits within your risk tolerance.

The First Principle of Successful Portfolio Allocation: Diversification

Who has not heard the old adage, "Don't put all your eggs in one basket"?

The point? Risk control. Risks are reduced by diversification. One basket might break, be stolen, or dropped. If your eggs are spread among a number of baskets, the odds of simultaneously losing all are significantly reduced.

How Does This Apply to the Stock Market?

Consider crowd psychology, specifically as it applied during 1999. The stock market had developed into a one-way street as stocks moved into the final phases of the strongest back-to-back two-decade bull market in history. During the mid-1990s, investor allure was focused on the Standard & Poor's 500 Index—a solid-enough group of stocks, even though their prices had far exceeded historical norms. Stocks had become extremely expensive based on historical relationships to corporate value.

By 1999, the public was ready for an even more speculative game—throwing capital at technology rather than at the quieter financial groups occupying large portions of the Standard & Poor's 500 Index. Oracle, Intel, Lucent, Microsoft, Texas Instruments, and Amazon, issues that largely traded over-the-counter, listed on the NASDAQ Composite Index, became the names to watch. Although the subsequent bear market was not widely recognized until 2000, it had already begun in many areas of the stock market as early as mid-1999. Broad segments of the market declined in price under cover of highly publicized speculative advances in the narrow groups of the technology sector.

Many portfolios became less diverse and more focused in narrow areas. At the same time, weakness spread in non-technology sectors. Eventually, as bubbles always do, the technology bubble burst in March of 2000, with the NASDAQ Composite Index eventually declining by more than 77%, not yet even one-half recovered as of 2008.

This market collapse was not a pretty sight. Many investors lost their life savings during the 2000–2002 market crash, as well as their retirement plans, and sometimes even their homes. Greed led many to concentrate and leverage investment portfolios in a few industry groups. For many investors of the period, eggs had been kept in one basket.

The Technology Bubble of 1999 Was Not Unique

Many bull markets end with bursts of glory for selected market sectors—gold, oil, airlines, bowling alleys, television producers, and Japanese stocks—all have had their days in the sun before collapse. Recent years have seen speculative run-ups as well, concentrated in emerging country stock markets such as China, Brazil, and Mexico. These bubbles can be fun—especially if you get in early, which is not the case for most investors. For the most part, you should approach the "hottest" areas in the stock market with care.

How and Why Diversification Works

Diversification means that your portfolio should have the following characteristics:

1. The components should produce relatively similar long-term rates of return, especially if returns are adjusted for risk level. (Lower-risk components such as bonds will produce less profit than higher-risk components such as stocks, but their extra safety justifies their inclusion.)
2. Components contain diverse long-term risk characteristics—some more risky than others, and some more risky during certain types of economic climates.

3. The price movements of the various components should be unrelated to each other.
4. There are times when different components rise and decline at the same time, just as there are occasions when prices move in opposite directions. If the price of one investment is not influenced by the price of the other, these are **uncorrelated** investments.

Examples

Investments made in Ford, Chrysler, and General Motors do not provide much in the way of diversification. Although these are separate companies, they are in the same industry, with their profitability and share prices increasing and declining, for the most part, at the same time. In a similar vein, the price movements of industries associated with auto manufacturers (such as rubber tires and battery manufacturers) are correlated with the price movements of major automobile manufacturers.

Investments in the London, Paris, and German stock markets do not provide very much diversification in relationship to investments made in the American stock markets because these European markets tend to rise and fall in close harmony with the New York Stock Exchange. There are times when European markets are stronger or weaker than the United States markets; **however, Far Eastern stock markets (China, Korea, Thailand, and Australia) have been relatively uncorrelated with the United States stock market and may provide diversification for American stock market investors.**

Real estate stocks and real estate proper produce long-term rates of return similar to those of the Standard & Poor's 500

Index but often at different times. **Real estate has been an excellent vehicle for diversification with the stock market.**

Gold rises in price during inflationary times, along with other commodity-related industries such as paper, mining, food production, and timber. These investments provide diversification within portfolios otherwise concentrated in high dividend-paying and finance-oriented stocks. Finance-oriented companies, as well as bonds, run into difficulty during high inflation, when commodities are favored. Gold prices soar during periods of inflation, which tend to be marked by rising interest rates, which adversely affect bond prices.

When interest rates fall, financial companies (brokerage houses, banks, and mortgage lenders) perform well in comparison to industries that thrive during rising inflation.

Consumer staple industries (food, soap, and household items) and defensive industries, such as health and drugs, perform well during slower economic growth, compared to industries that thrive best during strong economic growth (automobiles, airlines, trucking, and home building).

Diversification within your portfolios should be based on geographical factors, industry, and the rate of inflation.

Remember, "Don't put all your eggs in one basket."

How Diversification Performs Its Magic

Figure 8.1 illustrates the price movement of the NAREIT Index, which reflects the price movement of real estate investment trusts, the Standard & Poor's 500 Index, and a hypothetical portfolio rebalanced monthly to include 50% in the NAREIT Index and 50% in the Standard & Poor's 500 Index.

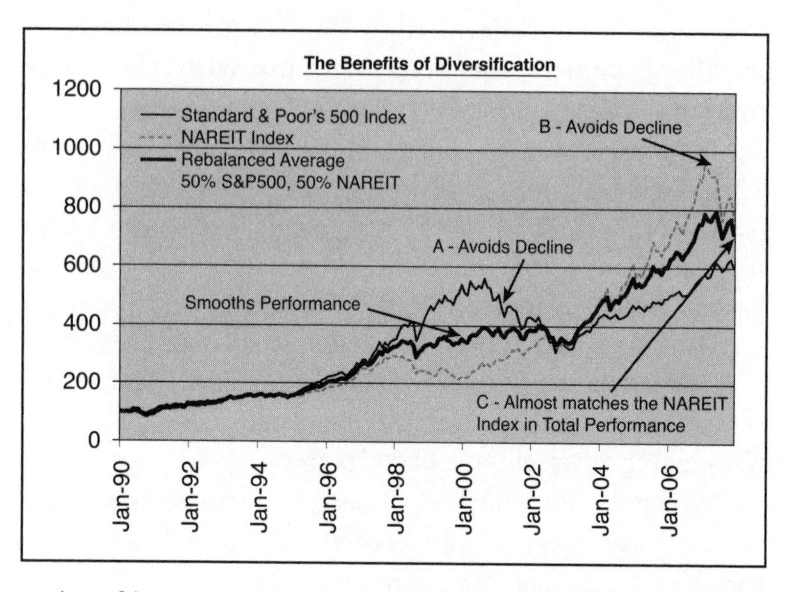

A portfolio maintained to start each month 50% in the NAREIT Index and 50% in the Standard & Poor's 500 Index provided, over an 18-year period, returns greater than the average of the two with less interim risk than either index.

Figure 8.1
An illustration of the effects of diversification within a stock portfolio.

The 1990–2007 period was favorable for both the NAREIT Index and the Standard & Poor's 500 Index. The Standard & Poor's 500 Index advanced at an average rate of 10.6% per year (including dividends), and the NAREIT Index advanced at a rate of 12.1% per year (including dividends). The average gain of a portfolio starting each month 50% invested in each, came to 11.67%—somewhat above the average return of the two areas, measured separately, which came to 11.35%.

(Diversified portfolios tend to do better than the average of their parts.)

Although both portfolios produced similar rates of return, each was subject to serious decline on its own, well beyond risk tolerances of most investors. For example, the Standard & Poor's 500 Index incurred a decline of 47.6%, based on weekly closing prices, between March of 2000 and September of 2002 (excluding dividends). The NAREIT Index had two serious drawdowns between 1990–2007—a decline of 23.0% between 1998–1999 and a loss of 21.2% during 2007.

By comparison, the diversified blend, 50% NAREIT Index and 50% Standard & Poor's 500 Index, had a maximum month-end drawdown of 16.8%, taken during September of 2002. The blend of real estate and the Standard & Poor's 500 Index captured 96.3% of the performance of the stronger of the two indices (11.67% for the blend, 12.1% for NAREIT), while incurring a one-time drawdown 27% less than the stronger area (16.8% versus 23.0% for NAREIT) and 64.7% less than the weaker area (16.8% versus 47.6% for the S & P 500). Risks of the blended portfolio were lower than the risks in each component of the blend because losses in the separate components of the portfolio did not take place at the same time, and were offset by either lower losses or by gains in the other component.

A High-Velocity Diversified Portfolio for Aggressive Investors

My management company, Signalert Corporation, maintains an aggressive diversified portfolio for certain accounts.

The management and composition of this diversified portfolio have consisted of the following:

1. Ongoing data is maintained regarding the strength of six industry sectors: utilities, energy, real estate, finance, health care, and Europe. We employ combinations of data sources, including www.steelesystems.com (Steele Systems) or www.morningstar.com, which provide information regarding the strength of market areas, as well as specific mutual funds.
2. On February 1 and August 1 of each year, we rank the performance of each of the sectors in the portfolio for the previous ten months.
3. The portfolio, going forward for the next six months, is divided into six units, based on the total asset value of the entire portfolio. (Each unit represents one-sixth of the dollar value of the account.) Two units (one-third of total assets) are placed into the best performing of the six sectors, based on performance the previous ten months. Two more units (one-third of total assets) are placed into the second-best performing sector, based on performance the previous ten months. One unit (one-sixth of total assets) is placed into each of the two next-best performing sectors, based on performance during the previous ten months. The two worst performing of the six sectors of each six-month period do not receive any assets for the next six months.

Here is the rationale behind this strategy: Investment analysts employ numerous techniques to outperform random selections. Market timing based on chart study represents one technique. The selection of stocks and bonds, based on analyses of corporate and industry fundamentals—earnings, value of assets, interest rates, and their effects on corporate profitability—represent another approach to stock selection. Selecting stocks based on past performance is a third approach, one whose merit is supported by research.

Professional market traders know that stocks, mutual funds, ETFs, and market sectors that have led in performance tend to maintain their lead in the immediate periods that follow. "Relative strength strategies" involve positioning investments in yesterday's leaders, which are likely to be tomorrow's leaders as well. (The same concept holds true in major league baseball, in which the teams in first place in early July are most likely to finish the season in first place.)

My own experiences have been favorable with "relative strength investing," and I know of many professional money managers who employ similar strategies. I suggest combining relative strength strategies with market timing strategies to secure the best of both worlds.

Putting Together Your Investment Portfolios

You can select investment areas to represent market sectors in which you may want to invest, for example, by following a diversified group of ETFs that represent specific industry groups. By tracking price movements of these ETFs, you can measure ten-month performance for your ranking of industry sectors by strength:

- **Utilities:** SPYDR Utilities (XLU)
- **Health Care:** SPYDR Health Care (XLV)
- **Europe:** iShares Europe (IEV)
- **Energy:** SPYDR Energy (XLE)
- **Finance:** SPYDR Finance (XLF)
- **Real Estate:** Cohen & Steers Realty (ICF)

For a very thorough discussion of exchange-traded funds, read *Investing with Exchange-Traded Funds Made Easy, Second Edition* by Marvin Appel, Ph.D. (FT Press, 2008), available at www.amazon.com. Marvin is my son, so you will have to take my word that bias is not involved in this recommendation. Check the reviewer comments on the Amazon site before you purchase it.

Numerous websites provide information on exchange traded funds. Search for "ETFs" or "exchange-traded funds."

Just to refresh:

1. Every six months (at the beginning of February and August), rank the six industry and geographical sectors by their strength during the previous ten months.
2. Redistribute assets for the coming six months, so that the two top-performing sectors each are assigned one-third of your assets. The next two sectors ranked by performance each are assigned one-sixth of your assets. The poorest-performing two sectors receive no assets for the coming six months.
3. This process is repeated every six months.

Past Performance

In my company's management of these accounts, we blend our assessments and selections of mutual funds specializing in specific market sectors with exchange-traded funds, ending with blends of portfolios with both mutual funds and ETFs at each six-month interval. This is a subjective process because final results are influenced by the ability of investors to select the best-performing representatives of market sectors (see Table 8.1).

Our research staff has hypothetically calculated that the following results would essentially have taken place if investors had employed a selection of mutual funds and ETFs that would have represented the market sectors that we are tracking. The investments that represented the two strongest of the six sectors would have been double weighted, the weakest two sectors excluded. Rebalancing would take place at six-month intervals

TABLE 8.1 *Performance Results of the Six Sector Strategy 1997–2007*

Year	Six Sector Strategy	S & P 500 Index
1997	+33.9%	+33.4%
1998	+11.2%	+28.6%
1999	+20.3%	+21.0%
2000	+19.7%	–9.1%
2001	+7.7%	–11.9%
2002	+9.0%	–22.1%
2003	+38.1%	+28.7%
2004	+23.4%	+10.9%
2005	+27.8%	+4.9%
2006	+28.1%	+14.1%
2007	+4.4%	+5.5%
Cumulative Performance	+632.5%	+136.8%
Compound Rate of Return	+22.0%	+8.8%

These results are hypothetical. The research includes data going back to 1988, but ETFs have been broadly available only during recent years.

The assumptions are that at six-month intervals, selections were made of mutual funds or, where available, ETFs, that represented sectors that had led the market for the previous ten months and whose performances had been exceeding the majority of mutual funds that invested in those sectors. To the extent that mutual fund selections have been retroactively determined, the past performance of this investment model, as shown, may have benefitted to some degree by the hindsight involved.

Figure 8.2 illustrates the ten-year performance of the six sector strategy for the period 1997–2007. The results are hypothetical.

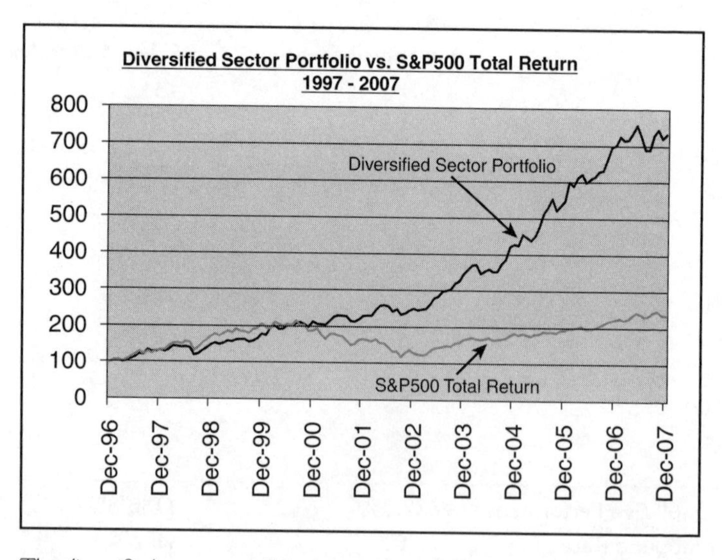

The diversified sector portfolio, invested on the basis of relative strength selection, almost consistently outperformed the Standard & Poor's 500 Index between 1997–2007, particularly as the twenty-first century began.

Figure 8.2
Diversified sector portfolio vs. S & P 500 Index total return (1997–2007)

Possible Variations on the Theme

At the time that my research staff conducted its initial research of diversified portfolios based upon relative strength, there were few exchange-traded and mutual funds available for an ideal portfolio. As a result, we limited portfolios to the six sector selections.

This is a narrow roster of potential candidates for investment and does not include all the potential areas available in the world of ETFs.

Four more potential candidates for your diversified portfolio roster might include the following:

- **An ETF for emerging markets (EEM):** Emerging market countries are less correlated with the United States stock market than are the markets of developed regions such as Europe, providing more diversification. The emerging economies of countries like Brazil, Mexico, China, Australia, and Thailand have greater potential for growth than the more established markets of Europe.
- **An ETF for the technology sector (QQQQ):** There are times when market areas represented by the Standard & Poor's 500 Index lead in relative strength, and times when technology issues, represented by the QQQQs, lead in strength. These frequently move in tandem, but they may also diverge.
- **An ETF for precious metals, a basic hedge against inflation—the gold ETF (GLD):** Gold is a volatile commodity whose price rises during inflation, uncertain global politics, and high interest rates. The gold ETF represents a ready way to participate in this precious metal, which also fits diversification.
- **An ETF for smaller companies, $250 million to $1 billion in capitalization (IWM):** This ETF represents a diverse group of smaller-cap American companies. Its action is consistent with United States stocks in general, but there

are times, often December and January, when smaller companies diverge in price and outperform larger companies.

If you were to blend this second group of four ETFs with the original group of six, your total universe would look like this:

Utilities (XLU)	Real Estate (ICF)	Small Companies (IWM)
Health Care (XLV)	Europe (IEV)	Emerging Markets (EEM)
Energy (XLE)	Technology (QQQQ)	
Finance (XLF)	Gold (GLD)	

This selection represents a broadly diversified portfolio.

The mode of operation for the ten-selection universe of ETFs might be the following:

1. Rebalancing takes place at six-month intervals, in February and August.
2. The top-three performing sectors for the previous ten months would receive double weighting and 20% of assets in each at the start of each six-month period. 60% of your sector assets are placed into the top-three performing sectors of the past ten months.
3. The next four best-performing sectors are each assigned 10% weighting in the portfolio. Sectors 4–7 in performance have a total of 40% of the portfolio.
4. The poorest-performing three sectors receive no representation.

5. A total diversified sector portfolio can be established to encompass between 10%–15% of your total stock portfolio and may be kept in motion, even during neutral periods, based upon Bond-Stock Valuation Models (including TWIBBS), and possibly even during bearish periods. If you always want to maintain moderate holdings in stocks, this is one alternative. However, this sort of portfolio during periods of market decline must be considered high risk.

(A close variation of this strategy, employing ETFs, is presented in Chapter 10, "Momentum Investing—Win by Going with the Flow.")

Summing Up

In this chapter, the benefits of portfolio diversification were explained:

- Principles associated with "relative strength"—buy the leaders and hold until they stop leading—can be combined with the principles of diversification to create above-average portfolio performance while reducing risks.
- Your risk/return performance is likely to improve considerably if you increase invested positions during periods when TWIBBS or other market timing models stand in their most favorable position.

CHAPTER 9

A PRIMER FOR PROFITABLE MUTUAL FUND SELECTION

To Have, to Hold, and to Trade: Some Super Playing Fields for Your Capital

If you have read this far along, it should go without saying that the growth and preservation of your investment capital rank high among your top priorities. The earlier you start accumulating capital for living expenses and retirement, the more you add to your investment base. This improves the odds that later in life, you will have the assets you need to enjoy the pleasures of travel and financial security.

This chapter examines specific areas to place capital.

Among the most popular of all investment vehicles in the United States are open-ended mutual funds. These provide liquidity and access to markets. Although mutual funds are popular, they do have their disadvantages, so consider the cons as well as the pros.

Open-Ended Mutual Funds: Professional Management, Ready Liquidity, Wide Choices, Popularity, But...

Open-ended mutual funds are created and operated by investment companies that raise capital from shareholders and invest with various goals, investment strategies, and under certain conditions. These "rules" are set forth in written prospectuses, which should be reviewed prior to making an investment. Choices for investors are more than plentiful. "Open end" means there is no limit on how many investors, shares, or dollars can go into the fund. In contrast, "closed-end" funds maintain fixed numbers of shares, which are traded among investors and not between investors and fund management.

Bond Mutual Funds

Funds that invest for income include those focusing on U.S. Government short-, intermediate-, or long-term bonds. Other bond funds invest in corporate bonds of higher (A to AAA rated) quality or in lower-grade corporate bonds (high-yield bond funds), which provide higher-interest payouts but involve greater risks of default. Some funds invest in longer-term bonds (more risk, higher-interest returns). Some stay with intermediate-term (five to seven year) bonds (less risk, lower-interest returns) or place investor assets in very short-term two to five year bonds or money market funds, which provide less income but minimum risk. In recent years, funds investing in foreign corporate and government debt have become more popular; their holdings may be denominated in foreign currencies, which may rise in price against the United States dollar, providing another avenue for potential profit in addition to income flow.

International Stock Funds

Gaining in popularity as well have been mutual funds investing in stocks outside of the United States. Until the past few years, the United States stock market has led other world markets, but recently markets in Europe and in emerging economies of Asia (not Japan) and South America have provided the best returns. The U.S. stock market represents one-half of the value of all stocks in the world. **I recommend that you maintain at least 25% of your portfolio in international mutual funds.**

Domestic Stock Funds

The largest number of mutual funds invest in domestic stocks, either exclusively or blended with international stocks.

The array of domestic equity mutual funds include those investing in large capitalization; blue chip stocks; technology-centered portfolios; smaller capitalization companies; gold, oil, and other commodities; and industry-specific portfolios, such as energy, finance, agriculture, and shipping.

All Buyers and Sellers Pay the Same Price Each Day

Open-end mutual fund investors indirectly own positions in the bonds and stocks of the fund portfolio. The fund share price is determined at the end of each day's trading, and is known as net asset value (NAV), or the value per share of the fund—the total value of assets held by the fund, divided by the number of shares outstanding at the end of each day. Buyers and sellers transact shares at the same price with the mutual fund, not with each other. If new shares are created, they are priced at net asset value, plus whatever entry fees are assessed.

Open-ended funds have no fixed number of shares that may be issued. Fund management creates more shares to meet new demand. Shares are retired if there are more sellers than buyers on any day. For the most part, transactions take place at one price each day—the price set after the next close of market trading at the net asset value per share—plus or minus any pertinent fees. (A few funds have allowed intra-day trading and pricing as well, but this has been the exception.)

Liquidity Has Been Broad and Flexible, But Not Without a Price

The mutual fund industry has had a fine record of meeting requests for redemption and their obligations to shareholders. Apart from some scandals that developed during the early 2000s regarding excess trading allowed to select investors, the industry has remained reliable, if not always particularly insightful, in its investment activities.

Mutual fund liquidity often does come with a price, however. Many fund families charge redemption fees as high as 3% of assets or even more, when made within specified times, ranging from one to three months to one year after initial purchase. Fees of 1%–2% for early redemptions, often initiated to discourage active trading, are frequent, especially for funds investing overseas. Selling commissions (called loads) are charged by many funds, usually at the time of purchase.

Many funds do not charge commissions but do charge ongoing fees to shareholders buried in the prospectus under "shareholder expenses," such as 12-b1 fees (fees charged to cover marketing expenses), which may be passed to brokerage houses as a form of sales commission.

Mutual funds meet requests for redemption readily, even if redemption fees are charged. However, during the credit crises in 2007 and 2008, some income funds such as Highland Floating Rate and ING Senior Income restricted redemptions by shareholders as per rights specified in their prospectuses, leaving many investors unable to close out their holdings.

Before making any fund purchase, verify the fund's redemption policies, entry and other fees, and the conditions under which fees are imposed.

Professional Management: Pros and Cons

Shareholders in open-ended mutual funds receive many benefits apart from ready liquidity. These include built-in diversification for even small investments, access to markets otherwise inaccessible to small or inexperienced investors, and economies of scale.

Shareholders are promised benefits of skilled management of fund assets. The cost of management is a large portion of fund expenses, which should be justified by the ability of management to outperform index funds.

Historically, this has generally NOT been the case. The majority of mutual funds have not outperformed portfolios designed to replicate the performance of certain market indices such as the Standard & Poor's 500 Index (index funds). Index funds do not attempt to select portfolios to outperform markets. Index funds incur fewer expenses than actively managed funds because A) they incur no costs for research or for portfolio managers and B) they have much less need to realign portfolios.

The remainder of the chapter discusses some fund-based strategies to improve your chances of outperforming market indices while meeting your investment objectives.

Invest in Funds with the Lowest Overhead

Mutual funds incurring the least expense are likely to outperform other funds. **Mutual fund expenses are passed along to the shareholders.** These include salaries of portfolio managers, transaction costs, research expenditures, housing and office facilities, accounting fees, and advertising. The typical stock mutual fund incurs expenses of 1% of assets per year, known as the expense ratio. Many funds report expense ratios as high as 2% and sometimes even higher.

The lower a fund's expense ratio, the better.

If the typical return of the market is 10% per year, and if you own a market-performing mutual fund with 1% per year in expenses, you lose 10% of your average profit each year. For your friendly mutual fund portfolio manager to simply match the 10% average return of the Standard & Poor's 500 Index on a net basis, he would have to produce returns of 11% per year before expenses.

Mutual funds run by aggressive portfolio managers who trade actively, turning over their portfolios by more than 100% per year, incur higher commission costs in the process. Frequent trading causes higher expense ratios.

Some mutual fund families are committed to reducing shareholder expenses as much as possible. The Vanguard family of funds, which is owned by its shareholders, has been among the most respected of fund families, because the expense ratios of its funds have remained among the lowest. The highly rated Vanguard Wellington fund has an expense ratio of only 0.36%. The Vanguard S & P 500 Index fund reports an expense ratio of 0.18% per year. Both of these are far below the average mutual fund expense ratio.

Where to Secure Information on Expense Ratios

If you search the Internet for "expense ratios of mutual funds," you will find websites of numerous mutual funds. You will also find many articles on the subject. Sites of fund families provide fund objectives, costs, past performance, and more—all worth checking out before making purchases. Even the SEC gets into the act, providing a free mutual fund cost calculator to compare all fees between funds (www.sec.gov/mfcc/mfcc-int.htm).

Tax Traps in Mutual Fund Investing

Mutual fund investors have to watch out for "tax traps" not applicable to individual stocks.

One trap arises at year-end. In profitable years, mutual funds may declare capital gain dividends, reflecting long-term and short-term profits taken during the year, as well as dividends and interest payments received.

These dividends, which are distributed to *all* investors, even to those who only recently purchased shares of the fund, are taxable. Investors receive notices of these distributions with copies sent to the IRS. These dividends reduce asset value in the fund because capital is removed from fund assets to be paid out to investors. So, the net asset value of your fund shares decline by the amount of dividends paid out. If you reinvest the dividend proceeds in new shares, these will have lower prices because of the decline in fund price. In the end, you will have the same investment value as you started with, but will have incurred a tax liability you might not have expected.

In effect, you have received a bill for income tax with no real profit.

To the extent that mutual funds do distribute such dividends to shareholders, as a taxable distribution, the ownership of mutual funds over the long term may involve taxes on capital gain, as well as income distribution, year by year even for long-term holders. This is a definite disadvantage, made even worse to investors who buy just prior to these distributions who have not benefited over the year from the gains upon which these year-end distributions are made.

In this regard, long-term investors may be better off holding individual shares of stock rather than investing in mutual funds.

Be very careful when you take new mutual fund positions near year-end, lest you fall into this trap. Before buying fund shares near year-end, check with the fund to determine when taxable distributions are scheduled. Hold off buying until after they have been made.

Star Ratings... Another Booby Trap?

Mutual fund families, especially following periods of rising stock prices, like to advertise historical performance records, as well as star (***) ratings of Morningstar, the very influential family of publications that reports on mutual fund composition and performance.

Although Morningstar provides valuable generic as well as specific information regarding mutual funds, the star ratings have had minimal success in predicting which funds will perform well in the future.

Do not be lured by star ratings into making purchases of any particular fund. Expense ratios are more likely to be a useful tool.

Strategies for When to Play It Hot and When to Play It Cool

Like the Las Vegas casinos, mutual funds provide tables for conservative investors and for aggressive investors.

Hot Funds

Some funds maintain "hot" portfolios subject to sharp price swings. These portfolios are often relatively undiversified, and overweighted with speculative companies with future prospects but not necessarily with assets or earnings today.

Such funds are "micro-cap (small company)," "growth technology," or "undiversified sector funds." Although their spheres of operation vary widely, some characteristics typical of "hot" mutual funds should be known in advance. They are highly volatile in their "beta" (price movement relative to benchmarks like the Standard & Poor's 500 Index); high, and sometimes very high. Hot funds provide the potential for fast gain—and also for serious ruin. (Remember how the heroes of 1999 fared in the disaster of 2000–2002?)

During most full market cycles, the extra returns by "hot and volatile mutual funds" do not justify the extra risks involved.

Funds That Are Reasonably Aggressive

There are a number of mutual funds whose portfolio values fluctuate more rapidly than staid market indices like the Standard & Poor's 500 Index. These funds invest overseas, in more volatile telecommunication, biotechnology, leisure, energy, or commodity areas. Sometimes, their portfolios are structured aggressively.

These mutual funds' beta may be 20%–50% greater than the Standard & Poor's 500 Index. (The majority of overseas mutual funds are also more volatile than the Standard & Poor's 500 Index, particularly those invested in emerging markets.)

It is a good strategy to confine the largest part of your equity mutual fund investments to funds of no more than average risk—probably funds with betas equal to but no more than 20% greater than the beta of the Standard & Poor's 500 Index.

There are times when mutual funds of greater-than-average volatility provide greater prospects than perils. When indicators like TWIBBS are flashing their green lights, and when Weekly Breadth signals and your Bond-Stock Valuation Models are in favorable position, these funds should be considered.

A favorable tapestry of indicator readings encompassing strong market breadth and positive interest rates, justify positions of 15%–25% in volatile, more dangerous, but strongly performing mutual funds—the percentage tempered by your risk tolerance.

Where to Find Beta Levels of Mutual Funds

For further information about beta, search on the web for "beta and mutual funds." Morningstar publishes an annual, *Morningstar Funds 500*, which provides a slew of information regarding each 500 fund covered, including the beta of each. *Morningstar Funds 500* provides 600 pages' worth of information.

Mutual Funds for All Seasons: Long-Term Consistency, Low Beta, Solid Management, Strong Performance/Risk Relationships

The performance of most mutual funds cannot be readily forecast based on their history.

However, certain characteristics of mutual funds have proven to be useful for predictions of future performance. Chapter 10, "Momentum Investing—Win by Going with the Flow," provides a strategy for the selection of exchange traded funds (ETFs) and traditional mutual funds. The five funds listed next were, as of the start of 2008, among my favorites for longer-term investment in portfolios for lower risk.

The fabulous five are as follows:

- First Eagle Global A
- First Eagle Overseas A
- Kinetics Paradigm
- Oakmark Equity & Income I
- American Funds Capital Income Builder A

First Eagle Global A: A Low-Volatility Global Equity Fund with an Outstanding Record

This is a conservatively managed equity fund that, as of the end of November 2007, held 25.6% of its assets in domestic stocks and 43.3% of assets in foreign stocks, 20% in cash, and the remainder in smaller holdings in bonds and preferred stocks. The fund invests mainly in developed countries such as Japan, France, and Switzerland, rather than in emerging markets.

With a beta of .59, the fund has been carrying approximately 60% of the risk of the Standard & Poor's 500 Index, but its returns, averaging 14.7% for ten years, 20.3% for five years, and 16.1% for three years, implies excellent upside potential despite what have been very small losses. Between 1998–2007, the worst year was 1998, when the fund lost 0.26%.

The expense ratio is just about average at 1.13%. *This is a load fund (5% maximum)*. First Eagle Global and First Eagle Overseas (discussed next) can be contacted at 800-334-2143.

First Eagle Overseas A: A Low-Volatility Fund That Invests in Foreign Stocks; Excellent Performance

A fund whose portfolio is comprised mainly of foreign stocks (71.7% as of late 2007), approximately 20% in income instruments. Major holdings have been in Japan (24%), France (16%), Switzerland (6.7%), and South Korea (5.6%).

An outstanding performance record—averaging 17.6% for three years, 22.7% for five years, and 16.5% for ten years. By comparison, the Standard & Poor's 500 Index had a 10-year return at the end of 2007 of just 5.7%. There were no annual losses between 1998–2007.

The expense ratio of the fund has averaged 1.12%. The drawback is maximum sales loads up to 5.00% of purchase outlay.

Kinetics Paradigm: A Growth Fund That Invests Globally but Carries More Risk than Other Funds in This Group

Kinetics has been an excellent performer (five-year average return through late 2007, +26.7%) with only one loss between

2000–2007 (–4.6% in 2002). However, its beta, at 1.19, indicates that it is 20% more volatile than the Standard & Poor's 500 Index. Its expense ratio of 1.63 adds a further risk, so Kinetics may not be suitable for all investors.

The price-earnings ratio of Kinetics is approximately 22—you pay $22 for every dollar of earnings in the portfolio. This is not horrendously high but is above those of the First Eagle funds, which have been around 18, which is roughly equal in early 2008 to the Standard & Poor's 500 Index. At the beginning of 2008, Kinetics was very concentrated in the financials (52.44%)—energy, consumer discretionary, and utilities represented another 37% of total holdings. The portfolio is not as widely diversified as the portfolios of other mutual funds. Management has, in the past, locked into a number of the strongest-performing industries, though the fund was hurt in 2008 by its holdings in financials.

The geographical blend of this fund is desirable—47.8% domestic holdings, 41.0% foreign stocks. A high-velocity vehicle with an outstanding record over a relatively short history, Kinetics is a higher-risk inclusion in the roster of favored vehicles, and is more suitable for aggressive as compared to more conservative investors.

There are no commission costs to buy the fund, but a cost of 2% is charged for redemptions within 30 days of purchase.

Kinetics can be contacted at 800-930-3828.

Oakmark Equity & Income I: Not the Highest Rates of Return in This Group, but Solid, Steady, and Very Consistent

A good vehicle to balance the potential hyper-nature of Kinetics, this large fund specializes in defensive and established industry groups (consumer discretionary, consumer staples, energy, industrials, and health)—48.5% in stocks (2007) and 34.4% in high-grade domestic bonds.

Oakmark Equity & Income I has been an ideal fund for investors with low risk tolerance. Its beta of 0.45 suggests risk levels less than half of the Standard & Poor's 500 Index—borne out by the performance of Oakmark Equity during the bear market—with gains of 19.9% (2000) and 18.0% (2001), and a loss of 2.1% (2002).

The fund is not likely to keep up with funds like Kinetics during bull markets, although its average gains for the three years ending 2007 (+11.2%), five years (+12.8%), and ten years (+12.3%) have well exceeded money market returns.

This fund is low-risk and suitable for long-term investment. Its beta, 0.45, is less than half the risk of the Standard & Poor's 500 Index; its expense ratio of .86 is below average as well.

The fund can be reached at 800-625-6275.

American Funds Capital Income Builder A: A Low-Risk, Geographically Diversified Fund with a History of Acceptable Return Coupled with Consistency

With a beta of 0.68, expense ratios of 0.55, a yield of 3.4%, and price-earnings ratio of just 15.36 (compared to more than 18 for the Standard & Poor's 500 Index), this fund merits attention for its safety. Investors had gains averaging 13.9% (five-year gains averaging 15.5%, and ten-year gains averaging 10.5%).

Capital Income Builder incurred only one loss between 1997–2007, a decline of 2.77% in 1999.

The fund's portfolio is well diversified—27% of assets in domestic stocks, 38.5% in foreign stocks, and 18.8% in domestic bonds (high grade). Stock holdings are spread among Germany, Australia, Spain, and Canada, among others.

The portfolio structure of American Funds Capital Income Builder A is not exciting—expect no fireworks. It is a fund for virtually every portfolio, with a consistent track record.

You can contact this fund at 800-325-3590.

Exchange-Traded Funds—An Alternative to the Traditional Mutual Fund

In recent years, a new form of fund has become increasingly popular with investors—the exchange traded fund or ETF. ETFs are similar to mutual funds in some ways, but different in others.

Most mutual funds provide active management of their assets. Exchange-traded funds are more like index mutual funds, and are not actively managed portfolios.

The issue with traditional funds is whether they provide expertise to outperform random stock or bond selection, particularly considering the costs of such "expertise" to shareholders. Some funds do; most do not.

Exchange traded funds do not provide active management of their portfolios, which are pre-set to meet specific investment objectives (for example, high dividend payouts). These objectives are to represent specific industry sectors (utilities, energy); to replicate market indices (the Standard & Poor's 500 Index or the Dow Industrials); and to represent geographical areas (Latin American stock market indices, European markets, emerging nation's markets, or country markets such as China, Korea, and Japan).

Sponsors design portfolios to meet the objectives of the ETF, and these remain stable and fully invested. There are no restrictions on the number of shares of each ETF. If demand increases, additional shares are packaged. If selling pressures overwhelm demand, sponsors close out shares.

Benefits to Investors

Investment expenses are lower for exchange traded funds than for the typical mutual fund, although not necessarily for index funds (such as those maintained by Vanguard). This favors ETF shareholders.

There are no redemption fees or limitations in frequency of trading with the ownership of exchange traded funds. Shares are traded on exchanges between investors rather than directly with the fund. Shareholders can buy and sell throughout the day, at the value of actual holdings established by the auction markets. This intra-day liquidity is prized by active traders, but comes at the expense of transaction commissions.

Active and savvy investors can change their portfolios in response to changing market conditions or in response to shifting strength among market sectors.

Chapter 10 provides strategies for the creation of portfolios of historical mutual funds and exchange traded funds, and shows how to combine portfolio allocation strategies with TWIBBS and other timing models to improve investment results.

Recommended Reading

Investing with Exchange-Traded Funds Made Easy, Second Edition by Marvin Appel, Ph.D. (FT Press, 2008). This is a fine introduction to the world of exchange-traded funds, including strategies for successful trading.

Internet Information

There are innumerable websites that provide considerable free information regarding ETFs. Among my favorites is:

www.etfconnect.com—A site that provides comprehensive information on the universe of exchange traded funds and specific ETFs.

For further sites, simply perform a search on the Web for "exchange-traded funds."

CHAPTER 10

MOMENTUM INVESTING—WIN BY GOING WITH THE FLOW

This chapter reveals two terrific strategies that enable you to create and maintain portfolios that will outperform the typical stock, mutual fund, and exchange traded fund.

These strategies have produced higher rates of profit than buy and hold, accompanied by **lower levels of risk**. Although the benefits are considerable, they are achieved with infrequent trading and low transaction expenses.

Relative Strength Trading in Mutual Funds

The following is a quick and dirty outline of the strategy for trading in the best-performing mutual funds:

- **At the start of each quarter, place capital into a diversified group of funds, each of whose performance during the previous quarter lay in the top 10% of all mutual funds in its class.**
- **Hold positions to the end of the quarter; then evaluate your holdings, keeping only those that have remained in the top 10%. Others are sold and replaced.**

- **This procedure starts each quarter with mutual funds leading the average.**
- **Your ongoing portfolios will outperform the typical mutual fund over the long term.**

To fill in some of the gaps, let's move on to the next section.

Monitoring, Selecting, and Maintaining Mutual Fund Portfolios with Superior Profit Potential and Risk Characteristics

The following are characteristics that separate consistent and strongly performing mutual funds from less-profitable ones:

1. The most consistently profitable mutual funds tend to be no more volatile than the Standard & Poor's 500 Index and are frequently less volatile. (For more information, review the recommended funds discussed in Chapter 9, "A Primer for Profitable Mutual Fund Selection.")

   Research shows that funds tending to move more rapidly than the average occasionally produce strong gains, but the risks are not justified by their occasionally higher returns.

   Create a universe of funds from which to select your portfolio components. The universe should emphasize funds of average to lower-than-average volatility.
2. At the turn of every calendar quarter, evaluate the performance of each of the funds in your universe. Identify those funds comprising the top 10% in performance.
3. From the top 10%, select a portfolio of five to ten funds. Your total fund portfolio should be broadly diversified—by industry sector (technology, health, commodity based), investment objective (income, balanced, capital gain),

capitalization level (large cap, small cap, mid-sized), and geography (domestic, Europe, Far East, emerging countries).

The maintenance of diversified portfolios of the best-performing funds adds considerably to the safety and performance level of your assets.

Summing Up the Process

At the end of each quarter, review the performance of the funds in your fund universe:

1. Funds in the top 10% of your fund universe are held.
2. Funds whose performances no longer lie in the top 10% are immediately sold and replaced.

This starts each quarter with a portfolio of funds stronger than 90% of all mutual funds during the previous quarter. Research shows that momentum is decisive. Funds leading in momentum outperform the average mutual fund.

Go with the momentum! Trade with the flow!

Filling in the Spaces

The following are details of some additional important components of this system:

1. Quarterly performance data of mutual funds is widely available, such as from *Barron's Financial Weekly*, or from many Internet sites, such as brokerage houses (Charles Schwab, T.D. Ameritrade, and Fidelity, for example). Newsletters and websites such as Morningstar provide—at relatively moderate cost—regular performance summaries of mutual funds.

Although there are thousands of mutual funds traded, you need no more than 500 mutual funds in your tracking universe to generate 50 funds comprising the top 10% in performance.

2. Your final selection is comprised of funds no more volatile than the Standard & Poor's 500 Index. You secure the volatility ratings of funds from sources such as Morningstar or via the Web. (Funds with volatility equal to the Standard & Poor's 500 Index have a beta of 1.0. Betas above 1.0 have greater-than-average volatility; betas below 1.0 represent volatilities that are less than average—a safer universe in which to invest.)
3. The minimum holding period of each of your funds is three months, although changes in market conditions might occasionally create situations where you change your holdings at more frequent intervals. Before purchasing any funds, verify if either the fund or your brokerage impose restrictions or extra charges for redemptions within 90 days from purchase. Verify that your fund selections may be redeemed after a 90-day holding period without penalty. There are ample funds to carry out this strategy.
4. Maintain full diversification in your fund portfolio. Although there are periods when specific industries will dominate in relative strength, well-diversified portfolios show smoother and less unstable results.

Performance of the Quarterly 10% Rebalancing Strategy over the Years

Figure 10.1 shows the growth of capital achieved by each 10% segment based on performance of a mutual fund universe with volatilities similar to or below the Standard & Poor's 500 Index. The highest-ranking decile maintained its lead in performance over other groups.

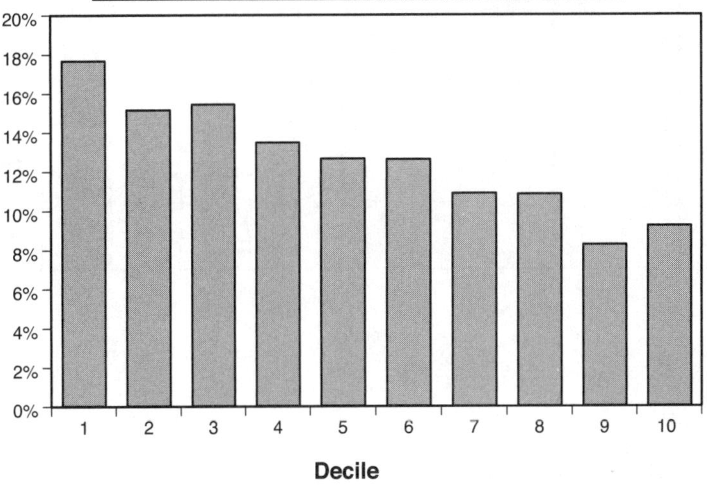

Funds in the top-performing decile, in the uppermost line, showed appreciation of 17.65% per year. Average funds showed appreciation of 12.6% per year. Funds in the lowest decile appreciated at 9.2% per year. (This is hypothetical performance.)

Figure 10.1
Growth of assets in mutual funds, grouped by relative strength decile rank, (1994–2007).

Figure 10.2 illustrates the performance of each decile in a somewhat different form—each bar shows the final values of assets theoretically invested in each performance decile.

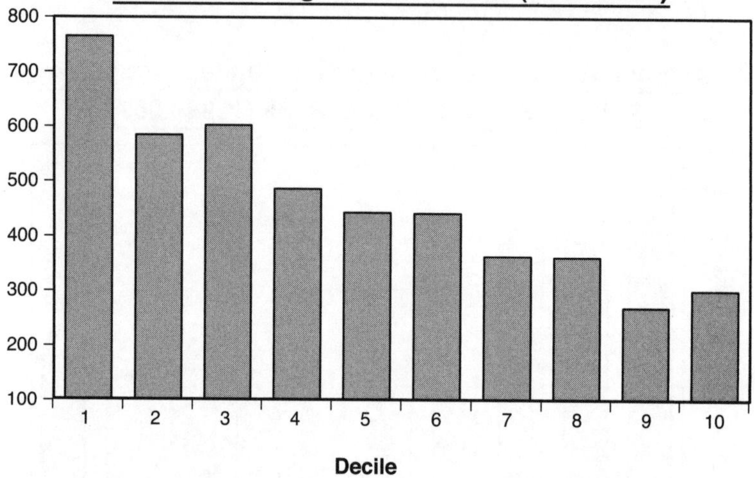

With the exception of deciles 2, 3, 9, and 10, the sequence of performance results is linear—the higher the rated decile, the greater its performance. Ninth decile mutual funds did not perform as well as mutual funds in the lowest decile; second decile funds performed slightly below third decile funds. Research has found that slight discrepancies of this sort sometimes appear, but as a rule, the higher the performance decile, the better the performance.

Figure 10.2
The cumulative performance of each mutual fund performance decile (1994–2007).

Evaluating the Final Investment Return in Comparison to Maximum Drawdown

Table 10.1 shows the compounded gain for each decile, the final amounts of growth, and the maximum drawdowns for each decile. Maximum risk is equal to maximum drawdown. **It**

is important to keep maximum drawdowns in your investment portfolio at as low levels as possible.

TABLE 10.1 *Performance Results by Performance Decile Mutual Fund Portfolio Mutual Funds of Volatility Equal to or Below Standard & Poor's 500 Index*

(November 30, 1994–May 2007)

Decile Rank	$100 Becomes	Gain Per Annum	Maximum Drawdown
1	$763	+17.65%	23.1%
2	$583	+15.14%	17.7%
3	$601	+15.43%	18.4%
4	$485	+13.46%	21.0%
5	$442	+12.63%	24.1%
6	$441	+12.60%	25.7%
7	$363	+10.86%	24.9%
8	$361	+10.82%	29.3%
9	$269	+8.24%	35.0%
10	$300	+9.20%	35.4%
Average:	**$461**	**+12.60%**	**25.46%**

Commentary

An investment of $100,000 in an average mutual fund achieved growth to $461,000, incurring a maximum loss of 25.46%.

An investment of $100,000 in the highest-performance decile of funds grew to $763,000, incurring a maximum loss of 23.1%. The net profit in Decile 1 funds, $663,000, was 83.7% greater than the net profit, $361,000, in the average mutual fund in this test universe. By following this rebalancing strategy, the compounded gain was double, compared to the average return over the whole period.

Risk levels were reduced by emphasizing funds of less-than-average volatility compared to the Standard & Poor's 500 Index. (Results, based on back testing, are hypothetical.)

Once More for the Road—Maintain Your Portfolios to Maximize Safety

This analysis represents typical risk/reward relationships when you reduce the volatility of your average portfolio components. Remember the golden rules: **Diversify, diversify, and then diversify further.** Avoid the temptation to chase after funds that have led the markets and that appear to be advancing in a vertical line (a parabolic advance). When these funds turn down, they may do so with a vengeance. Notice the higher risk levels in the highest-performing decile.

Funds recently entered into the highest-performing decile represent fine selections—their best days may only just be starting.

Another View of the Benefits of Relative Strength Investing in Mutual Funds

Figure 10.3 shows the slope of growth of assets, from 1994–2007, that was secured by investment in the top 10% of all funds, average funds, and funds in the bottom 10%.

Top decile funds outperformed the average and below-average groups consistently, with the slopes of long-term capital growth widening over time.

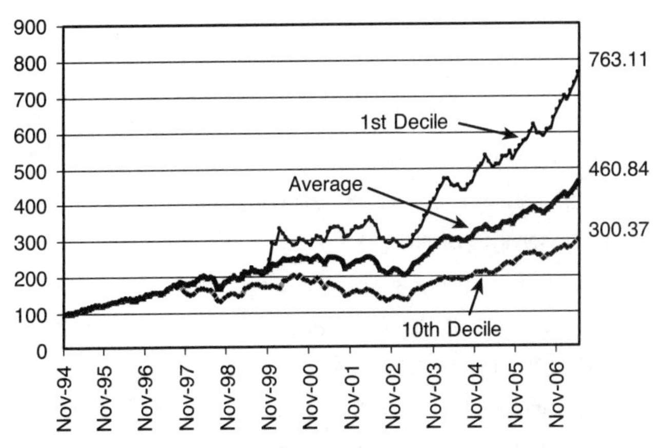

Funds leading the previous quarter continued to provide the greatest profit in subsequent quarters.

Figure 10.3
Slopes of growth of assets in the top decile, the average, and the lowest decile of mutual funds, rated by previous quarter performance.

Combining Mutual Fund Selection Strategies with Your Market Timing Models for the Best Risk/Reward

Investing on relative strength alone, staying with the leaders at all times, produces satisfactory results. Many savvy investors do precisely that. They invest on behalf of major foreign and domestic banks in currencies, commodities, stock markets. and bonds on the basis of price momentum—staying with the winners, and dropping others as their performance wanes.

But no one likes to see losses of 23.1% in their portfolio, even if long-term performance remains superb.

How can you reduce risk levels, while still following the leaders in performance?

Combine your mutual fund selection strategies with stock market forecasting tools like the Valuation Models and TWIBBS.

Take maximum positions when these timing models stand in their most favorable positions.

Maximum drawdowns are likely to remain low during such periods—for stocks in general, and for your relative strength-based portfolios in particular.

Do not hesitate to reduce positions should TWIBBS or the valuation models decline to unfavorable territory. Should stock market conditions decline from favorable to neutral, reduce equity positions or move assets into lower-volatility, highly rated mutual funds or into lower-volatility leading exchange traded funds until your tracking indicators improve.

Strike aggressively when market conditions are on your side, using these strategies to assemble "killer portfolios." **Reduce positions** to reduce risk as market conditions deteriorate. Investing on relative strength works best during favorable market climates. When bear markets dominate, even the strongest mutual funds decline because investors take profits.

How Relative Strength Investing May Be Affected by the Status of the Market Timing Models

Table 10.2 shows the relationship of portfolios of mutual funds assembled on the basis of relative strength (top 10% performers) and the status of the Twin Bond-Stock Valuation Model.

TABLE 10.2 *Performance of Top 10% Rated Mutual Funds in Relation to the Status of the Twin Bond-Stock Valuation Model (1994–2007)*

Status of Bond-Stock Valuation Models	% of Time Invested	Rate of Return While Invested	Maximum Drawdown While Invested
Both Bullish	38%	+28.6%	–12.5%
At Least One Bullish	65%	+24.7%	–12.5%
Both Neutral or Bullish	84%	+17.6%	–17.9%
One Neutral, One Bearish	19%	+10.6%	–16.9%
Both Bearish	16%	+11.2%	–21.2%

Commentary

Although mutual funds ranked in the top 10% tend to be profitable regardless of the general condition of the stock market, the best gains and the least risks take place during periods when the Twin Bond-Stock Valuation Models lie in favorable territory, with at least one of the two in its most bullish zone. The rate of return while invested, 28.6% per annum, highlights the combined power of the fund selection strategy and the Twin Bond-Stock Valuation Models. The preceding results (hypothetical back testing) reflect the selection of mutual funds no more volatile than the Standard & Poor's 500 Index.

Use these combined techniques regularly, religiously, and actively.

Creating and Maintaining "Killer ETF Portfolios" via Quarterly Relative Strength Rebalancing

Mutual funds are excellent vehicles for this strategy. However, their holdings are not as transparent as you would like, and liquidity limitations also sometimes cause concern—for example, when the stock market suddenly turns sharply down.

Consider dividing your assets into two portions: one placed in mutual funds, and the other in exchange-traded funds. The following is a strategy to identify the strongest ETFs at the start of every quarter.

The Top-3 Investment Strategies—A General Outline

The following procedures may be followed to create and maintain portfolios of exchange traded funds that are likely to outperform the general stock market.

- The stock market universe is divided into ten segments: seven domestic and three overseas.
- You review quarterly performance of ETFs in each of the ten market sectors.
- Capital is allocated so that one-third is placed at the start of each new quarter into each of the three sectors leading the ten.
- Positions are held for as long as they remain in the top three. As they drop out, they are sold and replaced by new entries.

The objective of this strategy is to maintain assets in the industry sectors leading in relative strength, and for as long as that remains true. Starting each quarter this way produces above-average returns.

The Ten Style Boxes in Your Portfolio

Selections are made from the ten areas representing a "style box," or investment option. Table 10.3 defines each of the ten style boxes, the market indices most relevant, and an exchange traded fund conforming to the investment criteria. This roster of ETFs is not inclusive. Familiarize yourself with the universe of exchange traded funds you may use in the Top-3 Strategy. As new ETFs are introduced, you can expect to have greater choices of ETFs to represent these areas, and an expanded ability to select the best-performing ETFs within each investment sector.

TABLE 10.3 *Menu of 10 Investment Options*

Investment Sector	Relevant Market Index	Available Exchange Traded Fund
U.S. Large-Cap Growth	S & P 500 Growth	ISF
U.S. Large-Cap Value	S & P 500 Value	IVE
U.S. Mid-Cap Growth	S & P 400 Growth	IJK
U.S. Mid-Cap Value	S & P 400 Value	IJJ
U.S. Small-Cap Growth	S & P 600 Growth	IJT
U.S. Small-Cap Value	S & P 600 Value	IJS
Europe	MSCI Europe	IEV or VGK
Emerging Markets	MSCI Emerging Markets	EEM
Far East	MSCI Far East	90% EWJ (Japan) and 10% EPP (Pacific ex-Japan)
NASDAQ 100 Index	NASDAQ 100 Index	QQQQ

This array includes liquidity, visibility, and diversification.

The areas represented are broad. This is not necessarily an advantage at all times but provides better diversification than investing in three specialized industry sector ETFs (such as those for energy, utilities, or financials).

Quarterly Rebalancing

Each quarter, secure the total return (price change + dividend payout) of each of the indices and exchange-traded funds. These are available from numerous sources like *Barron's Financial Weekly*, on the Web, or by calling the sponsor of each ETF. In addition, you can check sites such as www.ETFconnect.com, www.iSHARES.com, and www.sectorspdr.com.

Place one-third of your capital into the three ETFs of the 10 choices (the Top 3) that have shown the best performance during the previous quarter. Expect to take two new positions and to keep one from the previous quarter, on average.

The following summaries imply that you will be fully invested during each and every quarter, but make use of TWIBBS and the Bond-Stock Valuation Models to determine when you may want to retain assets on the sidelines. ETFs are always fully invested, unlike mutual funds, whose managers have the option of reducing investment positions by moving into cash. As a result, ETFs can be volatile, and may require caution.

Performance of the Top-3 Investment Strategies

Figure 10.4 shows the growth of assets traded via the Top-3 Investment Strategy compared to buying and holding all 10 indices.

Hypothetical Growth of $100 From 1996-2007

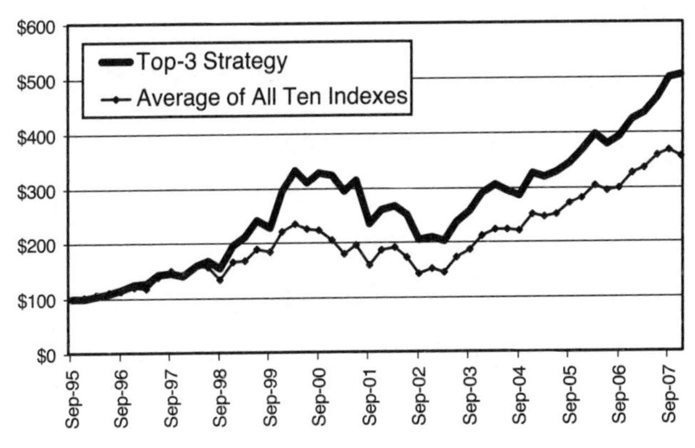

$100 invested at the start of 1996 grew to $503 by the end of 1997; an investment held in an average of ETFs representing the 10 sectors grew to $356.50. These results represented an annualized average return of 14.1% for the strategy, and 10.9% for random investment.

Figure 10.4

The Top-3 Investment Strategy; hypothetical growth of $100 (1996–2007).

Year-by-Year Performance:

Table 10.4 shows the year-by-year performance of the Top-3 Strategy in comparison to a buy and hold of all 10 indices, rotated each quarter to start with equal amounts of capital in each sector.

TABLE 10.4 *Annual Performance of Top-3 Compared to Unselected Performance (1996–2007)*

Year	Top-3	Average of 10 Sectors
1996	+25.6%	+18.2%
1997	+13.3%	+18.2%
1998	+38.5%	+16.5%
1999	+50.2%	+33.1%
2000	+9.6%	–7.3%
2001	–20.0%	–9.4%
2002	–18.7%	–17.5%
2003	+37.5%	+38.8%
2004	+12.8%	+17.6%
2005	+12.2%	+11.8%
2006	+15.9%	+16.2%
2007	+18.4%	+9.6%

The Top-3 Strategy outperformed the average of all indices during 26 of 49 quarters, achieving a compound return of 14.1% compared to 10.9% for the average sector in the group of 10.

The worst quarterly drawdown was 40% for both the Top-3 portfolio and for the average of 10 indices. This is higher than desirable, underscoring the importance of maintaining fully invested positions only in periods when TWIBBS or valuation models are favorable.

$100,000, compounding at 10.9%, grew to $472,000 over 15 years. $100,000, compounding at 14.1%, grew to $723,000 over 15 years. Improving rates of return by even moderate levels results in significant additional accumulation over the years.

Summing Up

This chapter explained two procedures to profitably employ in the selection of mutual funds and exchange traded funds that are likely to outperform the typical fund or ETF. Maintain the indicators from previous chapters and evaluate market conditions. Then decide whether to invest in stocks or the alternatives of mutual funds and exchange traded funds.

These tools should not be underestimated. They are powerful and effective.

The next chapter sums up with some observations of long-term planning and how these strategies fit with your personal plan.

CHAPTER 11

THE FINAL WORD

Summing Up Your Life Program of Accumulating and Enjoying Wealth

Reading and learning about investment strategies is one thing. Maintaining the discipline to carry forth these strategies is another.

The largest wealth is accumulated by market-savvy investors who develop their financial plans and follow their own smart rules.

First Step—Set Aside Investment Capital, Starting as Early as Possible and with as Much Capital as You Can Afford

The longer capital is compounded, the greater the benefit. An initial investment of $100,000, achieving a growth rate of 10% per year for 10 years, will grow to $259,460—a gain of 159.5%. An initial investment of $100,000 over 20 years, growing at a rate of 10% per year, will end the 20-year period at $672,750—a gain of 572.75%. By lengthening your investment period by 100%, you increase your profit by 160%. Such is the power of compounding returns.

Second Step—Add to Your Investment Capital Consistently

First Consideration: Your Personal Risk Tolerance

As your life situation changes—as you age, as your assets grow, as your ability to replace losses diminishes—reconsider risk in your portfolio.

During the early growth phases of your capital base, typical allocations might include 80% stocks and 20% income products. As your capital base increases, and as you age, you are likely to want to scale down the equity portion to 60% and perhaps as low as 40%, increasing income-producing components at the same time.

Some people, in their later years, choose to increase risk—but only with enough capital so that losses would be tolerable. Many people, once their essential needs are assured, temperamentally prefer to aim for greater rates of return. They want "to stay in the game." Others are content to coast along with safe, secure rates of return that meet their needs.

Keep your financial goals and risk tolerance in mind as you decide how to allocate your portfolio.

Assess the Risk Level and Current Climate of the Stock Market

Any forecasts of the future direction of stock prices are likely to be as accurate as those forecasts by "super experts." These experts write articles and books and appear on morning television—a new face every thirty seconds or so.

The establishment of financial columnists, portfolio managers, and financial analysts all have a vested interest in keeping the public optimistic and actively participating in the buying and selling of stocks. It is rare for brokerage houses to issue "sell" recommendations on stocks, with under-performers generally rated as "hold" rather than "sell."

With TWIBBS and the two Bond-Stock Valuation Models, you have the tools to time the market to match or surpass the performance of unmanaged market indices. You will also probably beat the performance of most market gurus.

The key is to buy and increase stock positions as TWIBBS and other market indicators flash the green light. Hold for as long as strength continues. Sell as market conditions weaken. It's really that simple.

Your entries and exits will not always prove accurate, but, on balance, your batting average should prove quite gratifying.

What Makes Investors Fight Their Own Best Interests?

In the absence of an advisor, why not have a meeting with yourself? Consider the price action of the stock market. Now, consider the decisions you have recently made. Do these decisions conform with your market indicators? Or, are you holding stocks falling in price because you cannot tolerate disappointment? Do your indicators imply improving strength rather than increasing weakness, or are you betting to the upside because you cannot tolerate the taking of losses in your portfolio? Do you enjoy trading too much to stay on the sidelines? Are you basing decisions on predictions by some television guru?

Maintain your own indicators. Create a plan of action. Follow the plan. You will not always be correct—that is a given. Always emphasize the preservation of capital. You should come out very well.

When the Overwhelming Majority Is on One Side of the Stock Market, It Is Usually Wrong

This axiom is easy to understand but hard to quantify, and almost always valid.

Suppose stocks have been rising for months or even for years—almost all investors are optimistic and believe that advances will continue for many years ahead. If everyone is optimistic, it follows that just about everyone is fully invested, with little cash on hand. Where is the money to come from to support further advances?

With prices already high, will you pay a premium for shares? Is the smart money still buying, or are companies and/or insiders putting new blocks of issues of their stocks on the market?

The moral? Disregard television. Disregard financial columnists. Disregard your friend's hot tip. Do *not* disregard the status of your valuation models and the status of TWIBBS. They will not be correct 100% of the time, but, based on past performance, the odds are in your favor. And, in addition, they have no axe to grind....

Finally, Use the Mutual Fund and ETF Selection Tools in Your Investment Arsenal

Trading in mutual funds and exchange traded funds on relative strength is not going to astound your neighbors or make you wealthy beyond your wildest dreams within a few months.

It is, however, likely to enable you to grind out above-average profits quarter after quarter, year after year, decade after decade, until your financial goals are achieved.

Combine powerful tools to select the best of investments and use indicators to time your invest decisions.

The rest will be up to you.

With my very best wishes to all....

Gerald Appel

EPILOGUE

June 30, 2008—Market declines have resumed, a major bear market is threatening...

Price pressures on stocks, during the first half of 2008, increased as the United States and foreign economies reeled under what appeared to be the start of a full-scale recession that, coupled with inflationary pressures, strained not just the country's lower income segment, but the higher income segment as well.

The banking industry has found itself struggling to survive in the face of widespread defaults by subprime borrowers, to whom excessive loans had been made as a result of widespread miscalculations of the risks involved. Bear Stearns, one of the more aggressive lenders, found its share price declining from $170 in mid-2007 to as low as $2 in March 2008, before recovering to $10. At this price, J.P. Morgan Chase was willing to purchase the company, and to assume (along with the Federal Reserve System) its debt.

The Federal Reserve Board has recently moved aggressively to support the banking industry in particular and the national economy in general by lowering interest rates, actually assuming the risks of billions of dollars of debt.

As I write, final outcomes remain uncertain. What is certain is that Bond-Stock Valuation Models, though weakening, remain favorable. This continues to argue against a major extension of the stock market decline. The stock market did recover a large portion of first quarter losses during April and May of 2008. However, this June appears to be developing into the poorest June since the height of the Great Depression in 1930. Stock markets are declining across major markets in Europe and Asia as well as in America.

The amounts by which stock earnings yields exceed yields from government bonds had, in late 2007 and early 2008, reached the highest levels in decades. In recent months, however, these gaps have narrowed.

These indicators, still bulwarks against ongoing market weakness, are facing many negative international and domestic adversaries: rising unemployment, broad inflation across the globe, weaknesses in banking systems here and overseas, and general angst and pessimism among investors.

Bond-Stock Valuation Models have been exerting a positive influence on the stock market, but now may or may not prove sufficient to forestall greater market declines than have ever taken place during periods of favorable readings.

For as long as Bond-Stock Valuation readings track in favorable territory, however, they should serve to limit market declines that would probably have been even more severe if not for their benevolent influence up to this point. Only time will tell....

The lessons for portfolio management:

- We have made the point that investors should maintain well-balanced and diversified portfolios at all times, with amounts of equity (stock) positions kept at levels commensurate with each investor's emotional and financial risk tolerances. Portfolios that maintain 60% of assets in stocks and 40% in income instruments would probably have lost no more than 10%–12% during the entire October 2007 to June 2008 decline, very possibly less if the stock selection strategies that you have learned had been followed.
- Careful portfolio balance does, indeed, help the cause. The two First Eagle mutual funds recommended in Chapter 9, "A Primer for Profitable Mutual Fund Selection," for lower risk investment actually declined by less than 3.2% (Global) and less than 2.7% (International) between January 1, 2008 and June 29, 2008, a period during which the Standard & Poor's 500 Index and the NASDAQ Composite Index declined by 12.9% and 12.7%, respectively.

The Final Word

There are times when it can be difficult to follow even the best designed plans, but one of the best lessons that can be taken from the stock market is that when the universal consensus leans one way, you can generally be pretty sure that the stock market is going to fool this consensus by following the other path.

Once again, for the final time, my very best wishes to all of you who have stayed with me from the start of this journey to the end.

Gerald Appel

APPENDIX

Performance Histories: Five Timing Models

In this appendix, the trade-by-trade histories of the timing models covered in this book are discussed. It would be worthwhile to study the following tables to get a good sense of the performance flow of the indicators involved.

The Baa Bond-Stock Valuation Model, 1982–2007

All Trades 1982–2007

Buy Date	Buy Price	Sell Date	Sell Price	% Gain	% Loss
820308	655.89	820405	698.29	6.46%	
820524	699.66	820614	668.79		–4.41%
820621	652.72	820628	669.21	2.53%	
820706	653.25	820719	671.85	2.85%	
820726	669.85	820907	735.51	9.80%	
841210	991.92	841231	1019.10	2.74%	
850107	1003.34	850114	1040.24	3.68%	
850617	1144.92	850624	1159.41	1.27%	
880906	1588.17	900312	1972.11	24.17%	
900326	1962.48	900402	1967.56	0.26%	
930809	2644.28	931115	2713.01	2.60%	
931122	2677.80	940411	2637.62		–1.50%
940822	2699.16	940829	2762.70	2.35%	
941128	2627.15	970120	4327.93	64.74%	
970224	4488.34	970505	4561.82	1.64%	
970519	4590.48	970527	4659.53	1.50%	
970714	5055.41	970728	5138.09	1.64%	
970804	5201.54	970811	5130.48		–1.37%
970818	5007.19	970825	5054.56	0.95%	
970902	5106.05	970908	5136.51	0.60%	
970922	5277.98	971006	5389.43	2.11%	
971020	5310.76	980302	5758.77	8.44%	
980831	5081.73	980928	5477.51	7.79%	
981005	5206.93	981019	5556.50	6.71%	
20010319	6303.74	20010402	6230.99		–1.15%
20030303	4709.38	20030317	4783.95	1.58%	
20030527	5367.44	20030721	5483.61	2.16%	
20030929	5685.35	20031013	5940.75	4.49%	
20031027	5870.18	20031110	5950.68	1.37%	
20031124	6016.09	20071231	9740.14	61.90%	
			Average	8.71%	–2.11%
			Average G/L	7.26%	

The Treasury Bond-Stock Valuation Model, 1981–2007

All Trades 1981–2007

Buy Date	Buy Price	Sell Date	Sell Price	% Gain	% Loss
811116	740.06	820201	719.12		–2.83%
820301	691.94	830314	919.81	32.93%	
841119	994.99	850211	1104.95	11.05%	
850422	1108.13	851111	1203.50	8.61%	
860407	1396.37	860414	1447.65	3.67%	
860421	1491.53	860428	1478.31		–0.89%
860721	1440.67	860728	1439.19		–0.10%
860915	1410.32	861117	1479.26	4.89%	
861124	1498.19	861201	1505.59	0.49%	
861215	1500.10	861222	1501.68	0.11%	
861229	1479.16	870105	1526.74	3.22%	
871207	1355.87	871214	1430.20	5.48%	
880229	1590.92	880314	1586.69		–0.27%
880328	1544.93	880404	1534.99		–0.64%
880523	1503.69	880531	1565.34	4.10%	
880906	1588.17	881024	1679.64	5.76%	
881031	1659.44	890103	1638.72		–1.25%
890703	1887.52	890724	1967.03	4.21%	
891016	2006.47	891023	2018.53	0.60%	
891030	1962.38	891113	1990.19	1.42%	
930308	2645.02	930322	2615.31		–1.12%
930329	2627.36	930524	2612.45		–0.57%
930601	2646.39	931115	2713.01	2.52%	
931122	2677.80	940214	2762.49	3.16%	
940228	2741.03	940321	2748.22	0.26%	
940404	2570.90	940411	2637.62	2.60%	
950306	2782.05	950327	2873.09	3.27%	
950403	2870.66	950410	2896.99	0.92%	
950424	2927.23	950501	2930.40	0.11%	
950522	2976.72	960318	3687.91	23.89%	
20010326	6206.89	20010423	6542.71	5.41%	
20010904	6233.74	20010910	6006.72		–3.64%
20010924	5513.35	20011126	6219.79	12.81%	
20011210	6114.26	20011217	6088.88		–0.42%
20020204	5949.20	20020318	6420.79	7.93%	
20020909	5172.03	20071231	9740.14	88.32%	
			Average	9.14%	–1.17%
			Average G/L	6.28%	

Twin Bond-Stock Valuation Model, 1981–2007

All Trades 1981–2007

Buy Date	Buy Price	Sell Date	Sell Price	% Gain	% Loss
811116	740.06	820201	719.12		–2.83%
820301	691.94	830314	919.81	32.93%	
841119	994.99	850211	1104.95	11.05%	
850422	1108.13	851111	1203.50	8.61%	
860407	1396.37	860414	1447.65	3.67%	
860421	1491.53	860428	1478.31		–0.89%
860721	1440.67	860728	1439.19		–0.10%
860915	1410.32	861117	1479.26	4.89%	
861124	1498.19	861201	1505.59	0.49%	
861215	1500.10	861222	1501.68	0.11%	
861229	1479.16	870105	1526.74	3.22%	
871207	1355.87	871214	1430.20	5.48%	
880229	1590.92	880314	1586.69		–0.27%
880328	1544.93	880404	1534.99		–0.64%
880523	1503.69	880531	1565.34	4.10%	
880906	1588.17	900312	1972.11	24.17%	
900326	1962.48	900402	1967.56	0.26%	
930308	2645.02	930322	2615.31		–1.12%
930329	2627.36	930524	2612.45		–0.57%
930601	2646.39	931115	2713.01	2.52%	
931122	2677.80	940411	2637.62		–1.50%
940822	2699.16	940829	2762.70	2.35%	
941128	2627.15	970120	4327.93	64.74%	
970224	4488.34	970505	4561.82	1.64%	
970519	4590.48	970527	4659.53	1.50%	
970714	5055.41	970728	5138.09	1.64%	
970804	5201.54	970811	5130.48		–1.37%
970818	5007.19	970825	5054.56	0.95%	
970902	5106.05	970908	5136.51	0.60%	
970922	5277.98	971006	5389.43	2.11%	
971020	5310.76	980302	5758.77	8.44%	
980831	5081.73	980928	5477.51	7.79%	
981005	5206.93	981019	5556.50	6.71%	
20010319	6303.74	20010423	6542.71	3.79%	
20010904	6233.74	20010910	6006.72		–3.64%
20010924	5513.35	20011126	6219.79	12.81%	
20011210	6114.26	20011217	6088.88		–0.42%
20020204	5949.20	20020318	6420.79	7.93%	
20020909	5172.03	20071231	9740.14	88.32%	
			Average	11.17%	–1.21%
			Average G/L	6.28%	

Twin Breadth Impulse-Bond Stock Valuation Mode (TWIBBS), 1981–2007

All Trades 1981–2007

Buy Date	Buy Price	Sell Date	% Sell Price	% Gain	% Loss
811116	740.06	820201	719.12		–2.83%
820301	691.94	830404	931.12	34.57%	
830411	941.80	830425	965.28	2.49%	
841119	994.99	851111	1203.50	20.96%	
851118	1211.01	860623	1487.62	22.84%	
860721	1440.67	860728	1439.19		–0.10%
860915	1410.32	861117	1479.26	4.89%	
861124	1498.19	861201	1505.59	0.49%	
861215	1500.10	861222	1501.68	0.11%	
861229	1479.16	870105	1526.74	3.22%	
870209	1679.43	870323	1806.31	7.55%	
871207	1355.87	871214	1430.20	5.48%	
880229	1590.92	880418	1551.91		–2.45%
880523	1503.69	880531	1565.34	4.10%	
880906	1588.17	900312	1972.11	24.17%	
900326	1962.48	900402	1967.56	0.26%	
910204	2011.97	910624	2151.75	6.95%	
930208	2612.45	931115	2713.01	3.85%	
931122	2677.80	940411	2637.62		–1.50%
940822	2699.16	940829	2762.70	2.35%	
941128	2627.15	970120	4327.93	64.74%	
970224	4488.34	970505	4561.82	1.64%	
970519	4590.48	970527	4659.53	1.50%	
970609	4759.98	980302	5758.77	20.98%	
980831	5081.73	980928	5477.51	7.79%	
981005	5206.93	981019	5556.50	6.71%	
981109	5912.20	990125	6196.84	4.81%	
20010319	6303.74	20010423	6542.71	3.79%	
20010904	6233.74	20010910	6006.72		–3.64%
20010924	5513.35	20011126	6219.79	12.81%	
20011210	6114.26	20011217	6088.88		–0.42%
20020204	5949.20	20020408	6255.84	5.15%	
20020909	5172.03	20071231	9740.14	88.32%	
			Average	13.43%	–1.82%
			Average G/L %	10.65%	

Weekly Breadth Signal, 1970–2007

All Signals 1970–2007

Buy Date	Buy Price	Sell Date	Sell Price	% Gain	% Loss
700908	478.67	701026	480.05	0.29%	
701207	517.48	710510	596.15	15.20%	
720110	604.50	720327	631.57	4.48%	
731001	617.72	731105	599.64		–2.93%
750113	406.45	750407	451.39	11.06%	
760112	539.15	760412	563.90	4.59%	
761213	595.83	770228	573.41		–3.76%
780807	615.39	780925	606.72		–1.41%
790820	655.78	791001	653.88		–0.29%
800519	649.12	801027	780.55	20.25%	
820830	713.94	830711	1030.30	44.31%	
850121	1069.22	850812	1149.05	7.47%	
851118	1211.01	860623	1487.62	22.84%	
870209	1679.43	870413	1714.42	2.08%	
880307	1591.66	880418	1551.91		–2.50%
910204	2011.97	910624	2151.75	6.95%	
920106	2430.37	920330	2357.84		–2.98%
930208	2612.45	931108	2693.34	3.10%	
970609	4759.98	971103	5208.94	9.43%	
981109	5912.20	990125	6196.84	4.81%	
20020107	6271.81	20020610	5851.40		–6.70%
20030428	5108.24	20030804	5515.68	7.98%	
20030908	5805.60	20040419	6620.05	14.03%	
20040830	6414.54	20050321	7229.20	12.70%	
20050620	7325.69	20050926	7556.45	3.15%	
20060905	8452.96	20070611	9841.73	16.43%	
			Average	11.11%	-2.94%
			Average G/L %	7.33%	

Commentary

As you can see, the various timing models do not produce signals with high frequency, but the signals that are produced carry high reliability.

TWIBBS is the timing model that provides the highest percentages of time in the stock market and that produces the highest rates of annual return. Its calculation does require additional time compared to other timing models, but, all in all, its consistency and performance do seem to have justified the effort over the years.

The Weekly Stock Market Power Gauge

As a quick and dirty—and very reliable—means of assessing the likely strength of the stock market, you can maintain the Weekly Stock Market Power Gauge, which is a measure of likely market strength marked by the status of the stock market indicators that you have learned.

The Gauge has levels that range from –3 (the most bearish) to +4 (the most bullish). As you might imagine, the most bullish levels are achieved when your strongest indicators are in their most favorable positions—positions generally marked by the greatest rates of gain and the lowest levels of risk. The most bearish levels of The Gauge develop when your indicators are in their weakest positions, marked historically by negative rates of return and/or the highest levels of risk.

The table below, based upon performance data, 1981–2007, shows potential combinations of indicators, rates of return and Gauge levels.

Indicator Combination	GPA While Invested*	Maximum Drawdown**	Gauge Level
Both Bond-Stock Models Bullish, Weekly Breadth Signal in Effect	+24.1%	–6.5%	+4
One Bond-Stock Model Bullish, Weekly Breadth Signal in Effect	+22.9%	–9.2%	+3
Bond-Stock Models Both Neutral or One Bearish – Weekly Breadth Signal In Effect	+25.09	–8.0%	+3
Both Bond-Stock Valuation Models Bullish; Weekly Breadth Signal Not In Effect	+18.9%	–11.1%	+2
Either Bond-Stock Valuation Model But Not Both on Buy. Weekly Breadth Signal Not in Effect	+17.3%	–18.8%	+1
Bond-Stock Models Both Neutral or One Bearish — Weekly Breadth Signal Not in Effect	+ 1.5%	–31.0%	0
Both Bond-Stock Valuation Models On Sell, But Weekly Breadth Signal On Buy.	–15.0%	–20.1%	–2
Both Bond-Stock Valuation Models On Sell. Weekly Breadth Signal Not In Effect	–9.4%	–36.8%	–3

NOTES:

* GPA While Invested—The annualized rate of return during the time you are invested.

** Maximum Drawdown—The largest cumulative loss taken during periods that these conditions have been in effect before new highs in profitability have been attained.

More detailed performance summaries appear in chapters of this book that introduce the above indicators.

As you can see, the greatest rates of return and/or the periods of lowest risk have taken place during periods in which the Gauge has stood at either +3 or +4. Negative rates of return and the greatest draw downs have taken place during periods in which the Gauge had negative readings.

Weekly Breadth Signals have been quite significant in the past and exert a strong influence

Upon the readings of the Gauge. Periods during which both Bond-Stock Valuation Models are in their most favorable position are also marked by favorable readings in the Weekly Stock Market Power Gauge.

Rules for Dealing with Combinations of Negative and Positive Numbers

In dealing with stock market data, there are many occasions where it is necessary to deal with negative as well as positive numbers. A negative number (for example, –5) might be thought of as a debit—a measure of value below "0." So, as one example, if you were to subtract –5 from +5 (5), the differential between a credit of +5 and a debit, –5, would equal 10. The person who has $5 in his pocket is actually $10 better off than a person who owes $5 (–5).

Most pocket calculators can be employed to readily carry out any operations that require negative as well as positive numbers. Hewlett-Packard business calculators are very adept in this regard.

The following are rules for carrying forth calculations involving negative and positive numbers:

- Adding two positive numbers results in the sum of the two numbers (4 + 4 = 8).
- Adding one positive and one negative number results in the differential between the two numbers, positive value minus negative value (4 + –3 = +1) (4 + –5 = –1).

- Subtracting a positive number from a greater positive number results in a positive number $(+5 - +3 = 2)$.
- Subtracting a positive number from a smaller positive number results in a negative number $(+5 - +7 = -2)$.
- Multiplying a positive number by a positive number results in a positive number $(4 \times 4 = 16)$.
- Multiplying a positive number by a negative number results in a negative number $(4 \times -4 = -16)$ or $(-4 \times 4 = -16)$.
- Multiplying a negative number by a negative number results in a positive number $(-6 \times -6 = 36)$.
- Dividing a positive number by a negative number or dividing a negative number by a positive number results in a negative number $(6 \div -3 = -2)$ $(-6 \div 3 = -2)$.
- Dividing a negative number by a negative number results in a positive number $(-6 \div -2 = 3)$.

Related Websites

The following websites may be consulted for further discussion regarding calculations involving positive and negative numbers

http.//www.squidoo.com/negative-numbers

http://math.about.com/od/prealgebra/ht/Positive.Neg.htm

INDEX

O–P

Q–R

S